JOBLESS AT 50

PALMETTO
PUBLISHING
Charleston, SC
www.PalmettoPublishing.com

Paperback ISBN: 9798822964686

JOBLESS AT 50

A BLUE COLLAR DIARY

RICHARD A. JOHNSON

TABLE OF CONTENTS

CHAPTER 1

EARNING THE FIRST CHECK

Well, let me start by giving you a little family background. I was born in a large southern town. I lived and still live on the west side of Jacksonville, Florida. We resided in the suburbs in a new brick home. I was the middle of three boys. I had an older brother who was seven years my senior and a younger one who was just shy of two years my junior. I was born a small child—real small. I was the smallest boy in school from grade school to middle school, until eighth grade. In class pictures, I was placed in the front desk for the picture, or you would not see me at all.

My father was a short man from the country. He was built tough and solid. He had moved to the city for work. He grew up during the Depression. He had a joke when asked what it was like growing up in the Depression. Was it depressing? He said would say, "I was too busy working that tobacco to be depressed!" When asked about how big his family was, he would say, "Let's see…Seems there were six of us brothers. And each one of us had two sisters."

Dad had a great sense of humor. He was proud of his family though. He said on many occasions we had nothing but each other, and that was enough. He grew up working the fields and earning his keep by the sweat of his brow. This finally gave way to the lure of a steady check and a smaller area to tend. He came to the city to get off the farm. He worked the night shift at a bakery that supplied a grocery chain. It made bread that fed much of the southeast. He also wrestled for extra cash at the Main Street Gym. So, in essence, though a ham and egger, Dad was a pro wrestler. He supported us and was a good father. As it turned out, he was a role model to many of the kids in our neighborhood. He always did the right thing in every situation and would sacrifice anything to help someone out.

My mother was a beautiful woman and was from a small town in the country. She too moved to the city for work and to find her future. That she did, and she excelled at it. She met my father, and they were married. This did not slow her down. Unlike a lot of mothers of that time, she worked and had a pretty good job. She was an assistant manager to a department store downtown and was well known by all the downtown patrons. She accomplished this by the time she was eighteen. She ran that store with an iron fist, and she ran our house the same way. Her mind was analytical. Mom would always get to the root cause of any problem. Then she had the tenacity to solve it. She was the one who dealt out discipline in our family, and she was tough. She loved us though and continued to do as much for us as she could until her passing. And I have yet to meet a more determined, smarter person.

Well, my story starts like that of so many other people my age. I started working as soon as I could get a permit to do so, and that was at age fourteen. My father told me at that time, "Son, once you earn that first check, you will always want one." I guess he was right. I was halfway decent at school. I loved English and writing, but like so many other people, I did not see a living at it. All I could see was my mother and father working their tails off, and there was still no extra money for the latest clothes for my time. I decided that if I wanted those things, I needed to work for them. Now before I could get a permit to work, I had my own little business. At age twelve, I had cornered the market on lawn care in my neighborhood. I had six yards. Yet that still did not deliver what a part-time job would, so off to work I went.

I started by throwing tires at a used tire company. They paid me what I weighed. A buck twenty-five an hour. Then a job came open at my mother's place of work. The Christmas rush was on. There I put together bikes, toys, and furniture and pulled layaways. When I was not doing that, I would help my brother wash gas station signs for a little extra money. He paid me well, and lunch was part of my pay.

I did well enough at the store to land myself a stock boy job. The manager was happy with my enthusiasm. That lasted until the store suddenly went out of business. This was much to my mother's dismay. It did little to stop her though. She was well known in the retail business downtown as a great assistant manager. Part of Mom's strength was her ability to employ a diverse group of folks and have the respect and admiration of all of them. Mom didn't care about gender. Mom didn't care about race. Mom didn't care about your sexual preferences. Mom didn't play favorites. And she demanded the best effort from everybody every day. So, it did not take long for her to be recruited by another store to run it. I, however, needed a new job.

I took marine mechanics in high school at the prompting of some of my friends. I learned what I could about small engines and outboard motors. After one year, if you made a B or better, you could get out of school to work. If you held a job in a related area, they gave you an A for the course and extra credits. Through a school contact, I landed a job at a golf course with a friend of mine. I went to the job with good intentions and a toolbox. I was supposed to maintain and repair lawnmowers. Somehow, that was not what happened. I wound up cutting grass all spring and summer long. Not what I had intended, but it paid the same, and I had a great tan.

That went along well. I had a buddy I rode with, and we left school every day at noon. We were off on Thursdays and Sundays and worked all day on Saturday. Then one day the groundskeeper asked me to follow him to the back nine so he could show me where I needed to cut. He pointed in a general direction, barked out, "Cut that!" and proceeded away on his golf cart. Now I did not know anything about golf at that time and had not bothered to learn. I knew my sections to cut and what height to cut them. I went after where I thought he wanted me to cut. I thought, Gee, this is tough going. I was using a push mower, and it was kind of high, but I attacked anyway with a passion.

When he came back, I had cut down an acre of rough, and now it looked like a fairway. He wasn't happy. Now that was the end of that. He did not fire me for it; he cussed at me. I took it even though

4

I thought I had done what he asked. He developed an attitude toward me after that. He never told me what I had done wrong; it was just a bunch of cussing. I worked all summer, six days a week. When school started the next fall, he came to me and said, "I need for you to be here at 4:00 a.m. Monday. I want you to turn these sprinklers on."

I did not have a car, and it was fifteen miles from my house. There was no way to ride a bike there and back and still get to school. He knew this, but I was told either do it or find somewhere else to work. That was the end of my golf course days.

CHAPTER 2

HARDWARE DAYS AND THE DIABOLICAL PLAN

So, I set out into a new adventure. I rounded up a job at a hardware store, and since they serviced lawnmowers, it fit my criteria at school. Just the ticket! I was getting paid and getting A's. I went to my father with what money I had saved, and using the golf course fiasco as an example, I was able to convince him to cosign for a car. It was a hotrod, a '73 Roadrunner. My dad told me at that time, "That car is where your paycheck is going to wind up." Of course, he was right as he was on so many things.

But that being done, I went into the world of hardware. This was back before the big chain store hardware days. Your local hardware store sold hardware, and that was it. They were lucky they had a small chain of four stores. Now, we did sell heaters, and this, for some reason, was my area of expertise. I took home all the paperwork on all our heaters and set about learning everything I could about those heaters. At the age of sixteen, I managed on a part-time basis to sell more of those heaters than anyone who worked in that small chain of hardware stores. I had the seller's gift. I did have some experience at selling though. I once won an award for selling more popcorn than anyone at my school. The award came not from the school but from the popcorn company. I sold so many cases of popcorn that even the kids whose parents were selling for them couldn't keep up. I even sold popcorn at an old folks' home to folks who had no teeth. So, I guess I did have a little edge. This was my way to the top. I quickly learned how to sell many items because I took time to learn my products and was nice to folks.

This went on as I finished high school, and I moved up to assistant manager. But the condition was a transfer. I wound up working for a guy in another store who soured me on the hardware business. He showed up every day mean and smelling like whatever he had drunk the night before.

One day, he showed up late, sat down in a chair at the front of the store, and just looked out of the window. Meanwhile, I tried to take care of a store full of customers. While I tried to take care of everyone, he called me from the rear of the store where I was helping a customer.

"Rick!" he screamed.

I ran to the front.

"Give me that book," he snarled at me.

He wanted me to push him a hardware book that was on a roll-around stand ten feet from where he was sitting. I was furious. I had a store full of customers, and this lazy, no-good son of a gun was just sitting there. With all I was doing, he wanted me to quit waiting on the customers and push him that book. Later that day, the district manager showed up. When he saw him coming across the parking lot, he tucked his shirt in, straightened up, and as soon as he hit the door started kissing up and taking credit for the things that I had been doing for him. Now I know it was wrong to have done this, but at that moment, I began to plot against him.

I realized at that time that working life was not always reaping the benefit of your own hard work. I did not learn this lesson well. Just about then, a friend told me of another opportunity at a dairy production plant. It paid better, so I applied and, after a short interview, landed the job.

It was time to put my plan into action. Since I had been working there, this guy had made it a practice to leave when he felt like leaving and go to a local bar right around the corner. He had told me to keep my mouth shut, as many Saturdays he would sneak out and go to the bar. He would leave and make me punch his timecard at the end of the day. The store managers were on the clock like everybody else. You see, in those days, you punched your timecard every day, and on Monday, they would be picked up. They would take the timecards to the district office and payroll would be done there. This Saturday, he left about two. Now the store was full, and it was time to get the party started.

It just so happened this guy's nephew, just a kid, was there that day. He worked part-time in the summer and did not know that store from a hole in the ground. And what's more, he let me know he didn't care either. I was told because he was family, he knew he would have his job there regardless of what he did or did not do. Now my unsuspecting manager had taken lunch at twelve. When he came back, he punched back in, and when he left at 2:00 p.m. for the bar—you guessed it—he ordered me to punch his timecard at the end of the day. Now it was the nephew and I in the store alone. What I did next was just for revenge. I could not help it.

I called my old manager, a delightful fellow named Bogey. I asked if he had any help in the store that day. He had told me yes. I exclaimed, "Bogey, I am quitting! I have had enough of this mean son of a gun over here You might want to come on over here and help this worthless nephew of my manager's. He's at the store, and his uncle is at the bar."

Bogey laughed out loud with glee. He had always hated that guy and had advised me not to go to that store. He already had an assistant manager, so when the job came up at the other store, I mistakenly went. Bogey said, "Okay kid, I will be right over. I told you this, didn't I?"

"I should have listened," I replied.

Now it was time to complete my diabolical plan. I then called the district manager and told him I was quitting. He wanted to know why. I said, "Maybe you ought to pay closer attention to your managers, like this one here you're so fond of. You will find him at Harpy's Bar around the corner from our store. You will also find a timecard that was punched back in at lunch and is not punched out for the end of the day. I was ordered today, as has been the case with many Saturdays that I have worked here, to punch that card at the end of the day. He has been ripping you guys off for a while."

Then it hit him. "Who is at the store?"

"Oh, don't worry; his bright little nephew is running the show!" I chuckled.

He said, "Rick, don't you leave that store!"

I replied, "Sorry, boss, you or this sorry manager you picked for me to work with have given me your last order."

With that, I hung up the phone, took off my assistant manager's vest, and chucked it across the counter at the kid. I said, "It's all yours, sport!"

The look on his face was priceless. I felt bad for the customers, but I couldn't help myself. I was getting even for months of mistreatment. If I had gone to the district manager, I would have been fired anyway because I let myself become involved. Had I gone to him in the beginning, maybe it would have been a different story.

Bogey came and saved the day. The district manager came and found the timecard. He then went to Harpy's Bar. Upon entering, the story goes he took a stool next to my wonderful manager and waited for him to turn his drunken butt around to notice him. When he realized that it was the district manager, he fell off the stool. He staggered to his feet, and at that moment, he was told that he was fired and "to take that worthless nephew with you when you clear your things out of our store."

I later learned of this entire story through Bogey. He and the district manager ran the store the rest of the day. He loved it; he told me it was the funniest thing that had ever happened in that hardware chain. Good old Bogey had been with them twenty years. They said I would never work for them again. So that was the end of the hardware business. It was time to move on to the next job.

CHAPTER 3

DAIRY PLANTS AND PAPER COMPANIES

So began my stint at the dairy plant. This place had you jumping through a variety of hoops to get through a day. When you first went in, you were sent to stack off ice cream onto pallets. You worked in the very coldest part of their freezer system. Then from there, you were, if you had some mechanical ability, sent to tear down the creamer machines. This was done so that hot steam could be sent through them to sanitize them. You, at that time in the same room, would change out all the O-rings and wash the parts you had taken off the machine. Then after the steam was done, you would reassemble the machine for the next shift.

At that point, you were sent to the ice cream area again to stack off for the next run. Then when you were through there, you went to the dry goods warehouse to finish out your shift sweeping. This was done in an area that had heaters in it to keep the supplies dry. If this does not sound like a lot of fun, believe me, it wasn't. After catching numerous colds, I decided that this probably would not be the best place for me to have a career. After two months, I began looking for something else. This job made me long for the hardware days. So, the search for bigger and better things was on the way.

On to the next endeavor. I learned a new manufacturing plant for paper products was opening. I went and sure enough received a job there. I started as what they called "a stacker." Stacking was accomplished by keeping up with numerous machines—fighting to keep up. This was by far the fastest job I had been into yet. I learned then production machines can wear you out, and they don't stop when you think you need to.

So be it. I poured myself into it and tried as hard as I could. I worked as fast as I could. After three months of me getting hammered, they came to me and said, "How would you like to learn to operate one of these machines?"

Well, I figured it had to be better adjusting on one than trying to keep up with one. So, I embarked on a journey to learn how to do just that. Now when this was going on, I discovered that manufacturing plants have their own little stories. These stories play out every day. Who was sleeping with whom? Who was mad at whom? Who was kissing the boss's butt? This one was on drugs. This one was drinking too much. The scenarios were incredible to me. Remember, I had just turned eighteen. I had not been around these kinds of soap operas before. I set myself the task of learning how to operate the machines. While I was doing this, I tried to steer clear of the turmoil around me.

Arguments frequently broke out, and the atmosphere was not pleasant. I had witnessed several fights, and it reminded me of school in a way.

I learned that grown folks could behave just like kids. I also pulled on something that I had learned in the hardware business. When people are riled about something, try to be diplomatic. Try to see their side, and then you yourself don't choose a side. On many occasions, I had satisfied an angry customer by doing just that. There would be times when I put myself on their side and agreed with them on a variety of issues. Be it a product or a fellow employee who did not treat them right. Once they felt I was on their side, I would commence to see if I could get them to see the other side of the issue. Often, I was able to do just that. I tried to employ this tactic now, and it worked well. I managed to stay in good working relationships while never picking sides—at least any that I vocalized. This I did carry with me.

Well, after a period, I had learned to operate a variety of machines, yet I was still a trainee. Then one day, I was offered a machine operator job. The catch was it was the midnight shift. Now I do not know if anyone who is reading this has ever worked the midnight shift, but it is a strange critter. The pros, in this place anyway, were that my machine and only one other ran that shift. We had the place to ourselves, and the second-shift supervisor instructed us at the end of his shift at midnight as to what was to be done and went home.

Now that did not mean that you could goof off. You were required to produce a predetermined amount of product based on machine speed. That, I later found out, could be manipulated somewhat if the machine was running well. You could get your production by simply turning the machine up past its normal running speed. This could get your numbers to look good at the shift's end. But if you pushed it too far, it would jam up. Remember, no one was watching us adjust the machine at night. A Jamaican fellow who was one of the other operators taught me this. Then there was the other thing: I did not have to deal with the turmoil on the other shifts. You did have days to get things done businesswise and such.

Now the bad part: I lived like a zombie. I never slept. I could not get used to the shift. I had, for my eighteen years, been a day person. Now I was being asked to be a vampire without the benefit of immortality. This went on for months. I got no sleep. Finally, I went to the day supervisor and asked if there would be an opening for a daytime job or at least a second-shift one. He was not sympathetic. I was asked if I wanted to go back to stacker. I knew that was not what I wanted to do. That would mean going backward. I was then told maybe I might be able to trade with one of the guys in training who wanted to be an operator. That meant going back to being an assistant operator—still backward. I thought for some sleep maybe I would do that; perhaps I could work myself back up. No such luck. No one wanted the shift. I was told after a while I would get used to it. That did not happen.

Now I learned another lesson that I would take with me throughout my career. Never ask to go backward, never, and don't go backward unless you're asked to. Very often, I found over the years that once you went backward, you were not likely to be promoted again. They would lose confidence in you and your ability to cope with new challenges. Now if you were asked to go backward to help the company out, that might be a different story. Then you're a *team player*!

My father, knowing I was not happy with my working schedule, began to look around for me an out. He found a guy who had a small construction outfit that needed a laborer. It was days, and that was all I needed to hear. I landed the job and gave my present company a two-week notice. Now, to the next lesson: once I gave my two-week notice, I was immediately moved back to stack off to finish out my next two weeks—unlike the dairy plant where I continued to do the same job until my notice was over. They were not happy with me, and it showed. They poured on the coals in hopes I would quit. I did not.

CHAPTER 4

THE CONSTRUCTION ENDEAVOR

So began my try at the construction world. Now this was strange to me. I went different places and was not contained within the confines of a building like I had been at all the rest of my jobs since the golf course. I was the only white guy on an all-black crew.

Now I was used to this though because I went to an all-black school for my fifth- and sixth-grade education. It seems I was part of the new desegregation process when I was eleven and twelve. Not only was I the smallest kid in school, but now I was one of about thirty white kids sent to learn how to get along with about three hundred black kids. There were other races there as well, but it was, for all intents and purposes, a black school. I am sure the black kids who were sent to the white schools felt as out of place as I did. I learned to get along with anybody though. Folks are folks no matter where you go. A sense of humor goes a long way when dealing with any type of folks no matter what the race or religion.

It has always served me well to find humor in different situations. I used the same tactics with the fellows I was with. Keep them laughing at you, and they will not find a reason to get mad at you. They acknowledged I was the first white boy they had worked with other than the boss, who, after all, was the boss so they had to get along with him. He was a rough character for sure. He spoke most times through a cigar at the corner of his mouth, and most of what he said was cuss words. He fussed at me and the other guys no matter what we did or didn't do. It flowed out of him like water. It seemed that it did not bother the other guys, so I did not let it bother me. I was told that was just his way, and I would get used to it.

Now before when I had heard that phrase, I had not been able to get used to whatever the person said I was going to get used to. We would see. In my working career, I had not heard anyone else speak quite like that to their employees on a regular basis.

The three men I worked with were as hard and tough as nails. There was Lavon, who was built like a bodybuilder. At that time, he would go six foot three and 225 pounds and was as solid as a rock. He was as strong as he looked and could do anything that he was put to task on. He had worked with the boss the longest and was a nice guy. Big Luther was bigger than Lavon; he was six eight and 275. He moved more slowly and did not do as much, but there were certain things he did better than Lavon. He had just a little better woodworking skill.

Then there was Roy. He was about six foot and 180 and was handy at concrete work and driving the trucks for materials. He was good at framing and could get into places to work that the other guys could not. That left me. I at that time was about five seven and 175.

I carried lumber, bags of concrete, and sandbags. Roofing materials up the ladder was always fun, especially in Florida in midsummer. I think though I enjoyed pushing the wheelbarrows of concrete the most. I was built for it. I was short and stocky so my leverage was good. I developed good relationships with these guys and worked hard to be one of the crew. We would go to this rough bar at lunch on Fridays to cash our paychecks. It was in a black neighborhood, and I never saw a white guy in the place but me.

The first time I went in, I went in with Lavon on one side and Big Luther on the other. Lavon shouted out for them to kill the music, which they promptly did. He hollered out, "Listen up. This here is Rick, He works with us, and he's cool." He continued, "We don't want him messed with when he comes in here, and that means with or without us."

Then Big Luther said, "Y'all got that?"

The crowd just sort of nodded their heads, and the music started playing again. It was as if I had been raised there. I was introduced to the owner of the bar. He cashed my check and kept five dollars for doing it, and I bought a pint of Jack Daniels for later. I never had a problem and could go in there with or without them after that. These men were respected.

Then as the months passed by, the work for our little company seemed to be getting slower and slower. Because of my limited experience, I started doing jobs on the property. The other guys went out alone on the jobs now. The owner ran his business out of his father's place. It had several houses and about ten acres of land. I was set about cutting grass and clipping hedges. It sort of reminded me of my golf course days. Then one day I was pulled into the rat's nest he called his office. He told me I was a good worker, but business was slow, and the other guys had been with him a long time. This combined with the fact they had also been in the business a long time spelled the end of the road for me.

This had been my fourth job since high school. The first three I had left on my own for different jobs, and now at a tender age, I was being laid off. This stung a bit. All this had occurred in just less than two years. Things at that point sort of went into slow motion for me.

CHAPTER 5

THE LIFE CHANGER

Even though I was only nineteen years old, I could see this coming and had figured out where I was on the pecking order. I knew I was vulnerable and had been looking elsewhere for work. I was very interested in this one company; it was one of the best-paying jobs in town. I had made it a habit that when I was let off early or we were rained out, I would go and apply. I began to show up on such a regular basis that the secretary up at the front office knew me by name.

This was in the days when you went to the office to fill out application forms. The following Monday after I was let go, I again went to the manufacturing plant. This time, I let the secretary know I was not employed anymore and asked if she could please keep an ear out for me. This place was a coffee, tea, and spice manufacturing plant. There was one other thing: it was a sister plant to the bakery where my father had earned his living for a great many years. He had no pull at the one

I was trying to get on at. The next Monday, I again showed up at the office and was told nothing was available.

When I went to leave though, the secretary told me in confidence, of course, that there might be an opening soon. She had heard that one fellow might be leaving. I thanked her and told her to please keep me in mind. I was willing to do any job they had if I could just get in the door. I knew it was one of the better places to work. Two more weeks and nothing every time I went back. I then began searching other avenues. I had moved out from home over a year before, and the thought of living back home was not good. The idea of going back home was to me like I had failed to make my way in the world. It came to a point where I really had started considering a military stint.

I liked being on my own and did not want to become dependent on my parents. Finally, I approached my parents and told them if something did not break within the next two weeks, I was joining something. It did not really matter which branch; I had to do something. Remember, I was nineteen, and I had to get working. It came to pass that in the next week, I went down to the recruiting office and searched out my options.

When I went to my parents to say I thought about becoming a sailor, I was met with strong opposition. They were not hearing it. They did not want me in harm's way. After the crying and lecturing went on, I let it go for that day.

I returned the next day and told my dad I was going. He insisted that I give my job search more time and not rush into anything. I said, "Okay, two more weeks," and moved my stuff home. I could no longer afford the rent where I was.

Out of the clear blue on a Tuesday morning of the second week, I received a call. The secretary on the other end of the line said there was an opening, and I should be there at 8:00 a.m. to be interviewed. I assured her I would be there. She told me, "Now this is an interview only, and there will be other people in here for the same job." She wished me good luck, and I thanked her for calling. The next morning, I was there when they opened the gates. I was dressed and ready when the gates opened at 6:00 a.m. The office did not open until 7:00 a.m., but when the secretary came to open, I was sitting on the steps. She looked at me and said, "You're a bit early, are you not?"

I said, "I know, but I prefer to be early. I will wait outside until you guys get in there."

She just smiled, led me up the steps, and told me to sit down in the lobby. After about an hour of waiting, I started seeing my competitors show up. They were older than me and had better clothes for interviewing purposes. Soon there were eight of us there waiting. About that time, the plant superintendent walked in, looked around the room, pointed to one of the other guys, and asked him to follow him.

At that moment, my secretary friend spoke up. "That fellow there has been here since 6:00 a.m. to talk to you. I think you should talk to him first."

He said, "Okay."

She winked at me, and I went. *Showtime*!

Now once inside, I knew I had to sell myself. I had to beat out the other guys. He asked me about my experience, and I was glad to tell him about the dairy plant and the manufacturing plant and that I had been a machine operator. I said, "The construction stuff was good work to start with. And our work dried up." I told him that was what I was doing while I was trying to get on there. I told him how my father would drive me down there when he needed to go to headquarters and let me smell the coffee. Headquarters were located just down the block from this plant. I told him that as a child I always wanted to work there. I only lived two miles from there. Then as I approached the end of my interview, I assured him that I would do whatever was necessary to get the job. I had no objections to cutting my hair or shaving off my thin mustache.

I told him that if I was only given a chance, I would learn to run every machine in the plant, and in the meantime, there was no one in there that I could not keep up with. The last thing he asked was "Do you think you're as good as anybody working here?"

I quickly told him, "Present company excluded, sir, I am sure of it. If you hire me, you can let two guys go."

The smile that came across his face when I said that is something that I will never forget. I had learned to be bold but not bolder than the person hiring you. I had learned from all that had led up to that moment to be confident, and it was better if you could get the boss to like you not just as an employee but as a person.

At that very moment, the plant manager walked by. He was a big man and looked tough. He was dressed to the nines and looked as sharp as a tack. My interviewer asked me to hold on a minute. He stepped out, spoke briefly to him, and handed him my application. He quickly scanned it. He then stared at me and walked to the door. He swaggered in like John Wayne, stuck out his hand, and said, "Hello.

My name is Mr. Johnson. I am the plant manager here. I hear you're pretty good, is that true?"

I said, "Hello. My name is Richard Johnson. It is a pleasure to meet you," and I just let this good man know "I can do whatever you need done around here. You better believe I will not let the name Johnson down."

He just grinned at me and said, "You better not."

How lucky could I be that his last name was the same as mine? I knew at that moment I had just hit a home run. He said it was good to meet me, and I assured him it was my pleasure. The plant superintendent walked out with him. Then they turned, and both looked at me and smiled. The plant manager nodded his head. When the boss returned, he said, "Okay, when can you start?"

It is funny in life how one thing—just one thing, mind you—can change your life forever. When that secretary stopped the superintendent from taking in the other fellow instead of me, that one thing, I believe, changed my life forever. Now not just for a while but for the next twenty-five years. So it began that I started my over two-and-a-half decade journey with this company.

CHAPTER 6

TEATIME

The day I started; I was told that originally, I was supposed to go on the evening shift for sanitation. Seems as though this other employee who was in the rotation shift wanted the solid night shift the sanitation crew offered. So be it. I went to work in the tea department. Two weeks on days and two weeks on evenings. The supervisor showed me in. He was a skinny fellow and was a retired sailor. He was sort of to the point, but still he had a nice way about him and a friendly smile. He introduced me to a lady who had, believe it or not, a beehive hairdo. Her name was Mrs. Watson.

This surprised me; it was 1980, and you did not see many beehives. Nevertheless, this tall, skinny woman led me over to what they called "the bulk tea line."

It was a machine that put tea into a tall carton for you to make your own tea with a strainer instead of a bag. You don't see that anymore either. My job was simple enough. She ran the machine. I put twelve of them in a box and taped up the bottom and the top. I put a stamp that had a code date and what was in the box on it. Then I stacked them on a pallet in a certain way. There you had it. I was making a decent living. Well, for the next two weeks, I worked on this line and did okay.

I was also taught how to check the weight of the product and load the machine with cartons to be filled. I learned to clear it when it jammed up and restart it. I had learned all there was to know about the bulk tea line. In the meantime, I watched the comings and goings of the rest of the crews.

At that time, there were three departments. Coffee was the most sought-after department; it was our main product. There was the spice room, which was probably second in profit. Then there was the tea room, where I now worked. There was also shipping and receiving. These were the forklift operators.

Each department had its own cast of characters. They came from a variety of ethnic backgrounds. They were male and female and black, white, yellow, brown, and red. There were folks from well-to-do families and middle-class and poor backgrounds as well. There were what I called the elite, and then there were those of us who worked there. The elite, in most cases, were the sons and daughters of the big bosses from headquarters who were biding time until their real careers took off. Some were still in college, and some were sent there to learn how real blue-collar people make a living. They needed that dose of reality before Daddy gave them the trust fund.

Then there were those who needed that job to feed and dress their families and cared nothing about advancement, just the Friday paycheck. They needed insurance and some sort of retirement to look forward to. Now I did not have a family and was one of the single guys working at the plant. There was a difference though. I thought if I worked as hard as I could and learned as much as I could that I could at least climb up into a higher position. I really wanted the white shirt that the supervisors were wearing. It was prestigious to me in my small world.

So, then I went to work. My next task was to learn what they called the "tag less" machine. I was then introduced to a red-haired woman whom I would know for the rest of my career at the plant. Of course, I did not know that then.

This machine had a seat or stool, if you will, that you sat at like some kind of milking machine. You put a bag under one chute with a flip clamp, and then you put another under the other chute with a flip clamp. You hit the bottom of the bags until you heard the air flap switch. That meant one bag was full. You quickly took it off, clamped on another bag, and kept hitting the other one. You set the full bag in a tray and continued going. This you would do for thirty minutes. Then someone else would take over, and you would use a seal machine with a foot pedal to seal the bags, put them in the box, tape them up, and stack them.

You would do this task for thirty minutes. This is where I started meeting the rest of the crew. There were six women and just one other man besides me. Now I have worked with a variety of people of all kinds. To this day, this was one of the hardest groups I had worked around. They openly choose sides against each other and quarreled with each other all the time. They were not young, that is to say, they were not twenty-year-old gals. They were mostly thirty and forty years old.

At that time, they had four other spots for you to rotate to, including two hand-packing spots, where you put the tea into the cartons by hand. There were also two more stack-off spots, where you put the cartons in boxes and stacked them on a pallet. I set about doing everything I did not think the ladies were strong enough to do. I lifted pallets and brought in boxes and anything to keep them satisfied with me being there. Those pallets could weigh as much as eighty pounds. I did things I was warned by other men in other departments not to do because in reality it was their job to do these things. The old saying was if you are being paid like a man, work like one. That was the way most of these guys saw it.

I had even started something of a problem. After a while, the other women in the other departments were complaining that the women in my department had someone to do the heavy lifting. They wanted to know why they did not. Now the supervisors and the superintendent had to get together to discuss this problem. The other guys were mad at me because I was now putting them at risk to have to start doing all the heavier jobs.

Now we had women who were very capable of doing some of the heavier jobs. We had a few who were strong, tough gals. That was the exception not the rule. I was then pulled into this mess and asked why I had started doing that. Who had told me to do this? Did one of the supervisors ask me to do this? Did one of the operators ask me to do this? I said that the reason that I did it was to reduce the risk of injury to employees who could not ask for help to lift these things because no one was available to do so. I pointed out that even though they were paid the same, no one asked anyone to sign a waiver on a weight limit. There was nothing defining that you must be able to lift a certain amount of weight. There were no set limits on how much you could lift or not lift. When did you need help? Often, when in a position to do so, I would do as much of the lifting as possible before rotating. I had opened a can of worms now.

The plant manager became involved and asked why the supervisors were not taking care of this before now. He pointed out that the new guy had not been there a month and had already exposed one of their worst complaints. Back injury in the women was one of their main causes for missed time and injury. This started a chain of events. No women who did not sign off that they could lift at least fifty pounds were hired from that point on. They were instructed to get help any time something was too heavy. Now the guys, who I really thought were being petty about this, were made to lift most of the heavy stuff. I was put on the newly formed safety committee. The guys did not receive it well. I thought I had made some enemies right away.

That did not bother me though because it had made me a hero with the women in the plant. I just put my head down and kept working. We had two operators in our area. One had the name Pleasing Happy Weathers. This is no joke; that was what this man's name was. I could not believe it at first, but that was his name. He was an odd-looking fellow who sort of looked like a snake that had swallowed a bowling ball. His otherwise skinny face had puffed out cheeks that looked as if he had a mouthful of something all the time. When Happy would get excited about telling you something, he would literally spit all over you. He was a good man though and very opinionated. But much wisdom did I gather from him. I just learned over the years to keep my distance when speaking to him.

The other was a woman who was a bit older. Her name was Edith. She took a liking to me, and it turned out maybe not to be a good thing. She had, it was rumored, slept with one of the night supervisors. Now I would probably not write this but to vindicate her. I saw no evidence of this, and I learned over my tenure that rumors were often started out of sheer boredom. Those rumors could be very hurtful. People did not care. The more outlandish the better.

In any case, she took me under her wing and set about helping me navigate through our department. I was told whom to confide in and whom not to. If I had a gripe about something, she guided me in how to go about solving my problem. Over the next two years, we became close. So if you have not already guessed, there was a rumor that we were sleeping together. In my mind, she was a mentor and a friend and coworker. There was no relationship beyond that.

We had three other old gals who had been there since the place had opened. They were a tight little clique. All three were harmless and went about their daily duties, and that was that. No engaging in rumors or mean talk. They kept to themselves and did not mix in the other activities after work or such.

We also had a blender, and his favorite activity was the spreading of rumors. He was a hardworking guy and well liked around the plant. His job consisted of blending the different teas together and using a series of conveyors and handles to transport the tea to the different machines where it needed to go. We all worked a swing shift that rotated every two weeks. The blenders and the quality control people did not. This made these positions desirable to everybody. These positions were hard to come by.

Ron the blender had one flaw: he was attracted to some of the younger girls on the other shifts. He had been married for quite some time and had a gorgeous wife, but there was something pulling him. I could see it and often had tried to stick my nose where it did not belong. I used to say, "You have a baby doll at home. Why do you keep trying to put yourself in a bad situation?" But alas he could not help himself. It was part of his personality, and no amount of reasoning would help.

We grew close and spent many a night drinking beer and eating what was a new thing, chicken wings. Yes, that was during the new sports bar era. Try as I might to warn him, it was all for nothing. Finally, a very young girl who was working her way through college came in. She, unlike the other girls, did not care that he was married. It came to pass that as time went on they dated, and it happened. He soon was asking for a divorce.

This, for my friend, turned out to be the beginning of a very rough time for quite a few years. It just so happened that while he was seeing this young college girl, his then wife became pregnant. He insisted she did this on purpose to keep him in the relationship. He then set about a course that took him down a long road of child support payments. He traded that for getting to chase women and was quite successful at it. That is just the tip of his story, but we shall press on.

CHAPTER 7

THE
STICKER SITUATION

Time passed, and I kept my head down and kept working. I steered as clear as I could of trouble. I spent my off time lifting weights. If I was not at work, most times you could find me at the gym hitting the iron. I did this as a kid, and it was still good for me as a young adult. It served me well, as it helped me do my job. It increased my strength and stamina. If I was called upon to go to other more physical jobs, I could do them with ease.

I once encountered a situation that would forever change my direction at the plant. It seemed that someone had forgotten to label some tea boxes correctly. The code was wrong on the boxes and did not indicate the correct price of the product inside. The problem was there were about one hundred of these pallets. They were already loaded on the trucks and were ready for shipping. In those days, you did not just call the store, and they would go into the computer and change the code. The solution was to send a sticker with the correct code to be put on every box of tea.

You had to physically take each case, cut a small hole in the top, and insert the appropriate number of stickers. When I came to work that morning, my supervisor approached me and said, "Rick, we need someone to go down there and get this done. The plant is in a tight spot. The stores are waiting on this shipment of tea. Mr. Johnson needs to get this done and done as soon as possible."

When he said Mr. Johnson needed it done, that was something I had not heard before. If he wanted it done, I knew it must be of the utmost importance. This was a real challenge for my physical ability and organizing skills. I went at it like I was going to war. I had two people they could spare to work with me. They give me two of the gals. I had one count out the right number of stickers and fold them and the other cut the slit and put the stickers into the box. I transferred the cases from one pallet to the other. I would then sling down a fresh pallet and do it again.

I worked so fast and hard I was waiting on forklifts to bring more pallets. When the gals tired out, I did it alone, and I kept doing it. They took breaks, they went to lunch, and they stopped to rest. I kept going at a pace that could not be caught up with. I was in the zone. Nothing mattered but what I was doing, and in my mind, I was helping my plant. If Mr. Johnson needed it done right now, it had to be important to the whole company. This was now a mission. Four years of packing tea and going through my routine now was forgotten. I was doing a job that mattered and really doing something to help my plant.

This was not going unnoticed. People were watching. The supervisors stood at a distance and watched. The assistant plant manager came, and he too watched. Mr. Johnson showed up with the superintendent, and from a distance, they both watched. I knew they were watching me even though they did not act like it. I kept up this pace until the end of the day. When it came time for me to go, I had done it: I had corrected the problem. This was done exactly at the end of the shift. I was bleeding at the wrists from handling so many boxes. My hands were cracked open because the boxes had dried them out. My clothes were soaked with sweat so much that there was salt on them. I picked up a broom and began to clean the area. Just then, a hand touched my shoulder. I looked up, and it was Mr. Johnson.

He said, "Rick, you've done enough. Let the cleanup crew get this." He smiled and added, "You pulled us up out of the hole, son."

I replied, "It was my pleasure. I will always do whatever I can to help this plant!"

"I know it, and the plant knows it. And don't think I won't remember what you've done here today."

Mr. Johnson had a way of speaking to you that was genuine and real. When he spoke, he meant what he said. I told him thank you, and when he left, I welled up with pride so much I thought I might cry. I, in my whole life, had never felt like that. I was overcome with pride. The closest thing was when I was twelve and made a touchdown in a Little League football state championship game. Sure, it was just a physical thing, but at the time, I felt like only I could do it. I had won the day, and at that moment, I would have done it all over again.

This day went down in plant legend, and it is one to this day I will never forget because it shaped the next twenty-one years of my life. Like everything else I had done before, this one particular act once again changed my direction.

Two weeks later, I was summoned to Mr. Johnson's office. When I entered the office, the coffee supervisor and the receiving supervisor were sitting in there with Mr. Johnson. I looked around the room and said jokingly, "What did I do now?"

They laughed, and then I was asked to have a seat.

Mr. Johnson then said, "We have a problem. We have two supervisors here, and they both want you to go and work in their departments. It is an all-day shift, and there will be a dollar an hour increase in pay no matter which department you go to. To solve this, we are going to let you make the choice."

I thought carefully and responded, "Mr. Johnson, may I speak with you in private?"

"Yes, you may," he replied. He then asked the two supervisors to go have a cup of coffee.

Once they were gone, I asked Mr. Johnson some questions. I first wanted to know which path would take me to more promotions and get me to my goal of supervisor. I then wanted to know where he thought that the plant needed me most. Then I wanted to know where he would like to see me go. The last question was where would he go if he were me?

He thought for a minute and said, "Both are the same age. In each department, you would have one person in front of you who would have more seniority. Consequently, they are not supervisor material, and they would not want the job even if it was offered." He continued, "Now, neither will probably retire for ten years, and for that matter, no other supervisor will either. If you go with Jim, you will receive extra pay and be made an assistant at some point. If you go with coffee, you eventually will become a roaster, and other than supervisor, that is the highest paid job on the floor. The rate of advancement would be quicker in coffee. The plant needs you in coffee and would benefit from you being there." He went on, "It is my preference that you go to coffee because it is my baby and our marquee product. I would feel better knowing you were there. That being said, if it was me, I would go to coffee, but this is your choice. I felt as if this decision was yours to make. Both supervisors want you. One will lose, and one will win."

Now, I knew he really wanted me to go to coffee, and I also knew a lot of guys had quit or would quit if they had to go to the coffee dump. This job was as tough as it goest with an average of fourteen tons of coffee being physically handled a day. I had blended a lot of products, and I had not ever done this job since I had been there. I also knew that Jim was a no-nonsense kind of guy. It was rumored he would be hard to work for. I asked if I could sleep on it. Mr. Johnson agreed, and I went back to work.

I confided in a couple of my coworkers, and that did not help. One went one way, and the other went the next. I was on nights, so I really did not sleep that night. I spent the night trying to figure out what I should do. All night in my little single-wide trailer, I wrestled with this choice as I sat in my beanbag chair. I watched one of two channels on my black-and-white television situated atop an old tea crate from work as I pondered this question.

The next morning, I went to have coffee with my dad. Of all the things about him that I miss, that was one of them. We both loved coffee, and I would often go by the old house to sit and drink a few cups. We continued that tradition until he passed away in 1993. As always, I valued his advice and submitted my dilemma to him. He thought carefully and sipped his coffee, making the sound that he always made at the end of a long sip. "Well, if it were me, I probably would go where Mr. Johnson wanted me to go. He all but told you to go into that department. He respects you enough though to have given you the choice," he said.

I then said, "Dad, this is really a tough job. I have heard of guys quitting when they had to do this job. I have even heard if they want to run somebody off, they put them on this job."

My dad replied, "I have not seen anything, yet you were not strong enough to do. The job won't last forever. You will move up, but it may take time. You put your mind to it and your will, and you will not be defeated."

I went to work that day and into Mr. Johnson's office, where he was smoking a great big old cigar, and said, "I will go to the coffee department for you and for the plant and maybe for me too!"

He looked at me and grinned. He said, "I knew that's what you were going to do. You start Monday. You will make me proud."

CHAPTER 8

THE COFFEE DUMP

So it began, what would from here on be known as my coffee career. I was brought to the blending area, and this fellow called the Whip set about training me. He had the nick name because he liked cracking the whip. He enjoyed driving the blenders hard. I could tell right off this fellow was not quite right. He was about six foot and solid, and that was from the coffee bags. He referred to the bags as if they were a living thing. He just wasn't quite there. In any case, he taught me the ins and outs of the coffee dump.

You basically had a blend sheet that you went by. You pulled the coffee bags down off the pallets. The pallets were set at a predetermined height to let gravity do some of the work for you and to save your back. You would cut them open with a sharp knife and with what we called a go-devil push them to the hole. A go-devil is basically a dolly or pushcart that has one handle instead of two.

The furthest bag from the hole would be about fifteen yards. With a running start, you would sling as much as you could into the hole. These bags weighed upward of 180 pounds and on occasion 200 pounds. The more weight you could get into that dump hole, the better. This meant less weight for you to lift to get it dumped into the blending system.

Now what was rough was the pace. You had twenty-five minutes if all was running correctly to pull down, open, and get two tons of coffee to the hole. At times they would run four roasters, and this would increase your speed to two tons every eighteen minutes. You had to kick it now. This job was as hard as I had seen yet.

At that time, there was a man working there who was the roaster. His name was Mr. Griffin, and he was a good man. What I did not know at the time of taking the job was that Mr. Griffin had cancer. This opening that had come up in the coffee department was because he was very ill. He warned me that the Whip would work against me in the department and that he was indeed a little crazy. Their plan was for him to move into the roasting position when Mr. Griffin could no longer work. The Whip could roast even if he burned the place down. He was due his shot; he had paid his dues. That was why I was being trained for the coffee dump. But before this could happen, they wanted Mr. Griffin to train me on the roasters. He was a master at it, and he taught me well. He also told me that staying out and partying all night and trying to be a coffee blender would not mix. He was right.

Time passed, and Mr. Griffin got worse. Now they did something in those days that you may not see today. He was allowed to work if he felt like it. Mr. Johnson instructed our supervisor to let him work as long as he could. If he came in and could make the day or two hours, he was allowed to do so. This allowed him his insurance and the best he could provide for his family. He finally passed on, and we all grieved for him. I will never, as long as I live, forget what he taught me.

So, Whip finally got what he was waiting for, the roasting position. By then, I was a full-time blender. We had a couple of the guys in my department who said they would not work with him, and he would try to make it hard on the blender. He enjoyed torturing whoever was back there. He had worked off and on as a coffee blender for some time, at least four years. The rest of the time, he roasted. Now one thing about being the blender, you would have to get yourself far enough ahead to give the roaster a break and yourself one. While you were gone to break, the roaster was supposed to blend half a round for you so you would not get behind. The Whip would not do this.

His goal was to whip you into submission. He wanted you to quit. He took great pleasure in staring at you from around the roasters and laughing at your struggle. He would intentionally stop, look straight at you, and just laugh. This action, dear readers and friends, infuriated me. I know it should not have.

One day, as he was continuing this behavior, I went to him and asked, "What's so funny?"

He said, "You will see when the winter gets on good."

I replied, "Look, we have to work together back here."

He answered, "You do your job, and I will do mine."

I had no choice but to go to the supervisor and say I didn't know what his problem was, but he was not doing what he was supposed to do. He was not relieving me for breaks, and he kept staring at me while

I worked. He is trying to mentally harass me. My talking to him had done no good.

This got me no results whatsoever. I then went to the plant super-intendent through the chain of command and made a complaint. I did not mind busting my butt. Being harassed as I was doing it was another story. He came over and had a talk with him, and for a little while, it stopped. He started relieving me for my breaks and quit staring at me. He resented it though, and before long, he was back to his old tricks. Now he was determined to get me out of there.

I was determined to stay. I knew he was nuts, and every chance he got, he proved it. He resented me so much he would not ask me for a bathroom break because he did not want to return the favor. One day, I went to what was our intercom system phone to call for another pallet of coffee. I spun around to see him relieving himself in a metal drum. I was shocked. I later went to my supervisor and asked if he knew this was going on. He said he had been doing it for years. I asked why this was allowed because it wasn't very sanitary and he was handling coffee after it was roasted. He just sort of said he would talk to him, and that was it.

I then thought, This needs to stop. It just wasn't right, and I had to handle those drums as did the janitor who dumped the trash. I then did something that made him hate me more. I went to the head of the sanitation department and told him he better check those metal drums before letting the janitor dump them. When he asked why, I said, "Smell one of them, and you will see why."

When he checked them, he knew what he smelled. Unmistakable, it was urine. He came to me and said, "Who has been peeing in that drum?"

I replied, "Well, let me see. There are two of us working back here, and I'm too short to pee in that fifty-five-gallon drum."

The sanitation guy was not happy. He went and retrieved the supervisor from up front, brought him to the drums, and said, "Stick your nose in that drum!"

He replied, "That's okay."

The whole time, the Whip was peeping around from in front of the roasters. He wasn't laughing now. The supervisor said he would take care of it, and the sanitation supervisor made it clear if this happened again heads would roll. Whip was made to shut the roasters down, load up the tainted barrels onto a pallet, and dispose of them. He then retrieved new barrels and never urinated, that I saw, in them again. Now he really hated me, but not as much as he would.

CHAPTER 9

THE CHALLENGE

Now for a while, I lived right and didn't go out much as I settled into the job. I remembered what Mr. Griffin had told me and tried to stay at home unless it was Friday or Saturday night. After a while, I decided I could test the waters a little bit. Some of the other guys would go out during the week. So even though my job was more physical than theirs, I thought maybe I could go out too. It would start innocently enough. Just a few beers with the boys after work was how it had all started. This led to one beer after another, though, and before you knew it, they were hollering last call. This meant going home, getting maybe four hours of sleep, and feeling like hell all the next day.

After a few times, I decided it was better that about eleven or so I bow out. I stuck to my rule for some time. Then one night, it happened: I fell in with the right group, and there I was singing at last call.

The next morning, I was awakened by daylight. This was bad, as I always left home to go to work before dawn. I leaped from bed, pulled on my pants, grabbed my shirt and boots, grabbed a Coke, and headed for the door. The trailer park could hear me leave as my Trans Am roared up the driveway to the street. I was burning rubber and praying that my mostly shop-ridden car did not fail me now. I sped down what was a straight shot to work, pushing it as hard as I dared and hoping that a train did not catch me on the wrong side of the tracks. If a train caught me, it was all over. I was lucky one did not.

I slid sideways into the parking lot, jumped from my car, and put on my shirt running all out to the loading dock. I had put my socks and boots on at a red light. I jumped with one leap onto the dock and raced to the time clock. I was forty-five minutes late. I could hear the roasters humming from outside as I was running to the dock. You see, Whip was doing his favorite game now. He had done it to many blenders, and Whip wanted to run me out.

That meant he would have to shut the roasters down, that meant no production, and that meant I would be hauled onto the carpet. This he hoped was what he would do to me.

I was down three rounds. That meant I was six tons behind and maybe a little more when I reached the blending area. I looked up to see that the glass on the hopper above the roasters was empty. I could hear the familiar sound of a few beans hitting the bottom of the empty hopper. There he was, the Whip, in all his glory. He grinned from ear to ear. He just knew he had me. He hollered back, "Somebody's going to the office today, just as soon as these roasters go down."

At first, I thought I would admit defeat. He had all four roasters going. I would just take the butt-chewing or whatever they would do to me. I did not think I could catch him now. I looked up and back at the boys up front, and they laughed too. I guess they thought he would have beaten me like he had the rest of them. He then came around, pointed at me and then to them, and made the throat cut sign.

That was it! I grabbed a rag, shredded it, bound it around my head, and dove into the dump. I did have the good fortune that I had left my dump hole half full. As fast as I think I had ever done it, I pulled, cut, and dumped the second half round. I sent it to the blender, letting it mix only slightly, just enough, and then sent it to the hungry roasters. While this was happening, I was pulling and cutting as fast as I could. As soon as my path was clear, I poured another full round in. I was in the zone. The madder I got, the harder and faster I worked. The thought of him beating me seared into my head.

The roasters hummed steadily; the Whip was on top of his game. He roasted as fast as he could. He bumped up the gas to see if he could squeeze out the roasts faster. Every now and again, he would look from around the front of the roasters to see me pouring it on. I was at a dead run when I used the dolly to move the bags. Bag by bag, pound by pound, and minute by minute, I was walking him down. I was blending with an unbridled fury. I was consumed by it.

It took me just over two hours to catch him. All the while, I was working at a breakneck pace. I finally got caught up and had extra coffee on the floor. I could resume a normal pace. I went to the front of the roasters to see a beaten man. He had never been defeated at this little game. Many a man had been written up or quit because of his tactics but not me, at least not this day. I screamed in a voice for all to hear, "Go to break, you son of a bitch! Maybe when you get up there, you can ask for another roaster to run so you can keep up with me!"

His lip began to quiver, and his hands shook as he grabbed his hat and went on to break. He was greeted with laughter and people saying, "What happened, Whip?" He did not see me there at seven o'clock and had bragged about what he was about to do.

Happy looked at him and said, "Couldn't beat that short rascal, could you?"

The other guys told the tale for many a year. It was part of my legacy. The Whip continued to resent me.

CHAPTER 10

ENOUGH IS ENOUGH

Well, the months passed by, and winter came. My battles with Whip had somewhat subsided. Then the big winter push came. Now I was an accomplished coffee blender, and I knew every trick in the book.

The hours poured on me like hail from the sky. The roasters were running nonstop and twelve hours a day; sometimes we ran seven days a week. This was what Whip had meant about wintertime. People drink more coffee in the winter, which means more production. Every day, I battled with the four roasters, and I told people around me I was on the tree of woe! This went on, dear readers, as I fought not to be overcome by this onslaught. There were days when I would pull and cut and dump twenty-one tons of coffee. That was forty-two thousand pounds moved and handled by hand.

The weeks turned into months, and still this continued. I had no days off for over twenty-one days at one point. I drank protein shakes, ate vitamins, and consumed as much food as possible. Then, after

thirteen weeks of fighting this, I began to get sick. I started to wonder if Mr. Johnson had done this to me intentionally. Why were they
working me this hard? I could feel myself breaking down physically
and emotionally. I was starting to think they wanted me gone. Mr.
Johnson passed me every day through the department when he made
his rounds. Did he not know this? Were they trying to run me off?

I came in one Tuesday, and I was on the verge of collapse. I was
sick. I had the flu or something close. I tried to keep up, but it seemed
no matter how hard I fought, I was falling behind. I kept at it though,
trying not to go back home. Then the Whip's break time came. He
gave me the break sign over and over. I knew though that if I gave him
a break, I would not be given any help in kind. This would result in me
letting him run out of coffee.

The supervisor came back. He knew I was struggling but said,
"You're going to have to give him his break."

I asked, "Do you think this once you could give him his break?"

Now he knew that this man still did not relieve me for my breaks
like he was supposed to. He looked at me and said, "No, it's your job
to let him go on breaks."

With that, I stuck my knife in a coffee bag, went to the front of
the roasters, and relieved him for a break. When he arrived back from
break, I walked up front and went to the supervisor. I said, "I am sick,
and I'm leaving." With that, I hit the clock and went out the gate.

Now it just so happened that I did not have my trusty Trans Am
that day. It had broken down and was at the shop. That morning, I had
caught a ride with one of the other guys who lived out my way. I tried
calling my girlfriend to come get me, but she was asleep. She worked

the night shift and would still be in bed. I had nowhere else to go, so I walked three miles to her house.

I rapped on her bedroom window until I woke her. She came to the door. I explained what had happened and asked if I could lie down until she went to work. She could drop me off at Momma's on her way to work, and Dad would take me to get my car. She agreed, and I went and lay down.

I was considering quitting. I thought, They are dogging me to no end and did not care if I quit or not. Of course, I was sick, and that was not helping matters any. I wrestled with it in my head. This was the best-paying job I had ever had, and now I was being forced out. Had I been sent to the coffee dump to be run off? These thoughts continued as I finally drifted off to sleep.

Some three hours later, I was awakened, and my girlfriend said it was time to go. With fever in my head and feeling terrible about myself, I went to the old house. She dropped me off and left for work. I made my way into the house to find my dad eating a baloney sandwich and drinking sweet tea, watching some show on TV. I was greeted with "What are you doing here, boy? Why ain't you at work?"

I looked at him with sad eyes and said, "I can't do it anymore, dad. I think I am going to quit." I held my head in my hands as I said it. I was ashamed of it, and I was so sick.

He asked me what was wrong. I told him then what I had been going through. He asked if I had talked to my supervisor, and I told him yes.

"Then how about the superintendent? Have you talked to him?"

I again answered yes. I told him, "They just don't care." I didn't know what I had done to make them want to run me off.

He thought for a minute and said, "Maybe they are just seeing how much you will take."

He again looked off and back at me. The last thing I ever wanted to do was make him not proud of me.

He reached over and felt my forehead. Then he said, "You're burning up." He asked, "Have you taken anything for that fever?"

I said, "No."

He went into the kitchen and returned with a couple of aspirin and a tall glass of water. "Here, take these, and let's think about this for a minute," he said.

He then retrieved a wet wash rag from the bathroom and gave it to me to wipe my face. He told me to sit tight, and in a little while, he brought me some chicken broth to drink.

I drank it down, chasing it with the water. I felt a little better with every sip. It was opening me up and making me feel better. This day, Dad was off, and Mom was at work, so he was doing the mending and curing that day.

I told him I thought I had done all I could do. There had to be a better way to make a living. I did not know what, but I could not keep up this pace forever. I then said, "I think I will go and give notice tomorrow."

Dad then sat down across from me in his recliner.

He started, "It just seems a shame to waste almost five years of work because of this."

I replied, "Dad, I don't know. I don't see a way out." I continued, "I was told that is where they sent people to run them off."

He said sharply, "Maybe some folks but not you." He continued, "Ask yourself this: why, if you have done a good job so far, would they want to rid themselves of a good worker?"

I just shrugged my shoulders and shook my head. He arose, walked to the window, and looked out at the street. He then turned and said, "Someone might be taking advantage of the fact that it takes a lot for you to finally get upset and speak up." He then went to the kitchen and refreshed my ice water. He encouraged me to drink it down. He then said, "Before you decide to quit, you need to speak to Mr. Johnson."

I said, "Dad, he must know. He passes me twice a day back in that dump."

He responded, "Son, he has a whole plant to run. Could be he's not paying attention to your situation. Give the man a chance to make it right. He has not let you down so far."

I nodded. Then Dad took me to get my car and gave me some nighttime cold medicine. He hugged my neck and told me to go home, get some sleep, and talk to Mr. Johnson.

The next day, I found myself at work and back at the dump. My fever had broken, and I felt better. I had been given some strange looks by my supervisor, but he did not question me. I guess he must have known what was coming.

That morning, I continued to do my job, and at 8:30 a.m., right on time, Mr. Johnson came through. When he did, I was ready. I approached him and asked if I might have a word with him.

He stopped and said, "Yes, son, of course."

I leaned on my go-devil and began with my questioning. I asked how long I would be asked to keep blending for twelve hours a day behind four roasters. I then asked him if he saw any relief for me anytime soon. I followed with "I will blend until I drop if I can just see daylight. It might get me through. Also, why am I not getting relief for breaks?"

He then asked, "How long have you been blending behind four roasters for twelve-hour days?"

I replied, "Thirteen weeks now."

He continued "Have you had to work all the weekends we have worked as well?"

I answered, "Yes, sir, I have."

"Why are you not getting relief for breaks?"

I said, "Whip will not cover for me when I go on breaks."

He asked, "Have you talked to your supervisor about this?"

I said, "Yes."

His face turned red as he turned his gaze to my supervisor. He looked at me, put his arm around me, and pulled me close. He squeezed me a bit and said, "Son, you have been mistreated and it's my fault. I thought you were getting relief all this time. You have blended by hand over three million pounds of coffee. I am going to have somebody's ass."

I knew I had blended a lot, but three million pounds?

He gripped the back of my neck the way he would do and said, "I will take care of this."

I felt a mix of emotions and distrust for my supervisor.

When he approached the front of the department, the superintendent was there as well as my supervisor. He just pointed at them and waved his finger for them to follow him. When he was through, I went home in eight hours or was relieved to do an easier job. I was always relieved for a break. When filling up for a new blend, I was given help to do so. I would only have to keep up with four roasters by myself for short periods of time. My supervisor and the plant superintendent apologized to me. The plants superintendent told me that I was to come to him from then on, and he assured me my problems would be taken care of.

Turns out nobody had ever had to do what I had done. The fourth roaster was not supposed to be used. It was installed as a backup. It was supposed to be used to roast out at the end of a run, not as a regular tool. This had something to do with a labor study. Whip used it to keep up better and as a tool to punish his blenders. My supervisor, rather than give me relief, chose to dog me rather than make the other guys mad. They would get mad for being put back in the dump.

I learned some good lessons. Number one, first, never walk off the job and say, "I quit." Say, "I don't feel well and leave." Even though I was sick, the thought crossed my mind to say, "I quit." Had I done that, I would have lost my job and would not have learned the truth behind the situation. Think about it first. Number two, if you do not get results from one person, keep trying, even if you must go to the top. Better to go down swinging than just give up. The third thing is self-preservation. You must look after yourself, or nobody else will. Never trust someone else to decide what you can take and can't take. Fourth, stand up and be heard. It's better to have folks a little mad at you than to let something eat you up inside. Being heard before you quit something is a good idea. Fifth, trust your parents always. Not one person on this earth cares more for your well-being than your folks do. Maybe your wife or husband might care as much. In my case, I now have a wife who does, but that has not always been the case.

I am always saddened that I no longer have my father to confide in. His advice was always honest. Sometimes it was not what I wanted to hear. On more than one occasion, he had played devil's advocate. He always made me try to look at every side of a situation before deciding on it. He had done that this time, and it kept me working. I had survived the worst of the storm.

CHAPTER 11

FIRE IN THE HOLE

After making it through that winter, I settled in and was taken better care of. I resumed lifting weights on a regular basis and was healing my body. In the meantime, I took advantage of every chance I could to roast the coffee. I had learned one thing that the Whip had not. I knew how to attack a roaster fire. A roaster fire was a dreaded thing.

On occasion, the roasters would catch fire for a variety of reasons. Either they developed too much soot, something backed up, or there was a stack fire. This would happen when too much excess would build up close to the afterburners, fall in a huge fireball down the stack, and catch the roaster on fire.

The last kind was the worst. If you added too much coffee to a roaster, this would cause the cylinder to quit. If it quit, a twelve-inch-diameter gas pipe would feed fire to it until the whole thing ignited. You could burn up seven hundred pounds of coffee in no time. If it burned too long without being put out, when you realized the problem, reset the roaster, and turned it on, it would cause an explosion. There was a major flaw in the newly installed roaster panels that did not cut off the main flame when this occurred. The old roaster controls would not let this happen. I knew this, but I could not get them to understand what was happening since the flame was manually put out by the time the mechanics got involved.

I noticed something from the time of my first roaster fire. While the mechanics and operators jumped in, the Whip would not. I jumped in and did what I was told to extinguish the flames. You did not need much to fight a roaster fire. A water hose, an adjustable wrench, and a pair of asbestos gloves were all you needed—that and the guts to get close enough to the roaster while it was on fire. You had to take the wing nuts off the pipes to get inside the roaster. You could then spray water in it to put the fire out. All the while, fire would be shooting out of different areas of the roaster.

Now the Whip would stand back, his lip would quiver, and he would not get close. I saw from the start he was terrified of it. He was the roaster, and it was his job to put the fire out.

So as time passed, I sort of took the lead when a fire would break out. I figured out to more quickly put the fire out, you could use the emergency spray from on top. These were pipes that were positioned over the stacks to spray water down the pipes in the event of a fire. Before, they were only used when there was a stack fire. I figured out after watching the fire climb to the roof through the stacks, it was better to turn them on and let them keep spraying. It flooded the roasters with water and helped to slow the progression of the fire. This made firefighting easier.

On one occasion, I had left for the day, and the Whip stayed to roast out. He was clearing the system for the next run. He finished for the day and went home. When I arrived the next morning, I found out the fire department had been there the night before. The roasters had caught fire while we were at home. The night watchmen discovered it and called the fire department. In the meantime, he called the supervisor, and he followed shortly after the fire department arrived and told them how to put out the fire.

It burned up two of the roasters pretty good. The insulation was charred, and there was a huge mess on the floor. A couple thousand gallons of water running through sooty pipes will tend to do that. I was surveying the mess, and that was when my supervisor noticed something. The dust on the beams was smoldering. It had crawled all along the rooftop. There were little embers of fire everywhere. I had to take a brush, climb into the rafters, and crawl down each one to knock the fire off. Meanwhile, the Whip mopped the floor.

When I came down, I started looking for the source of the fire. One of the things I tried to do was learn where the fire came from. In this way, maybe I could prevent it from happening in the first place. It looked as though it had started from the bottom and climbed up. I then pulled one of the firebox covers to see that there were debris and old beans in the box. This was where it had started. Each day after the run, this stuff was supposed to be removed and put into a fireproof container. Even in the event of a fire, the boxes should be clean unless it occurs while you are running. At that time, a fire could occur from anywhere. If there was debris left in the box overnight, it would slowly catch the roaster on fire. The evidence was there. The Whip had not cleaned the firebox, and later the embers had spread to the rest of the roaster. It then climbed up one stack, fell down the other, and caught the next roaster on fire.

When I arose from checking the firebox, I looked over and saw the Whip nervously watching me. I could see guilt all over his face. He knew what had happened, and now he knew I did too. Just about that time, my supervisor asked me if I had found anything. I looked at the Whip and then back to my supervisor. I then said, "No, I didn't. No telling where it started."

Now I could have had his job right then and there. He was negligent, and it almost caught the whole plant on fire. He had surely done enough to me that not a soul would have blamed me. At that time, I had a forgiving heart though and had mercy on the Whip. Had the shoe been on the other foot, he would not have done the same. That was not how I was raised. I was raised to be forgiving. The manager at that hardware store was a different story. The Whip wasn't all there, and the things he had done I wrote off to him not knowing any better. The manager at the hardware store was a hateful and mean man. I did what I did to him because he had it coming. He was a thief and deserved what he got.

Things remained the same between me and the Whip. You would have thought that this act of kindness I had just committed would have changed the way he thought of me. I thought this would change things between us. He still resented me, and we still did not have a good working relationship. He still looked at me with hate in his eyes and openly spoke ill of me to other people. He had not beaten me down with the roasters. I had taken action to stop his mind games and ruined his plans of running me or the next guy off. I had ambitions, and I could run the roasters and blend coffee better than he could.

I had found out that he had been raised at a boys' home. He had been raised an orphan and never was adopted. I guess it had hardened his heart and done something to his mind. I tried to let it go and just keep plugging. When we had a fire or he had a problem with the roasters, I would be right there beside him to help him out. Until just now, I never told anybody about the fireboxes.

CHAPTER 12

THE ORIGIN OF RICK RANGER

Well, I thought to omit this part of the story, but it was part of my persona. It sort of became my nickname and stuck for the remainder of my time at the plant. How it happened was I had bought this 1984 Ford Ranger right off the showroom floor. I had traded my Trans Am in for it, and for the shape the car was in, I did not get beat too badly on the deal. One afternoon, after a rousing coffee-blending session, I decided to go to Mom's and eat supper with the folks.

On my way, I passed the elementary school where I had attended grade school. I looked to my right into the schoolyard and saw against the fence a truck on fire and children all around it.

I threw the Ranger into low and hauled tail around to the nearest gate.

I entered the playground and saw there were children everywhere. Someone had stuck two bales of hay under the truck right in the gas tank area and must have lit it. I screamed at the teachers to get the kids back. They, in excitement, wanted to see what was going on. The frantic teachers were at that point trying to get them back with little success. I looked for anything I could use. The paint had melted off the sides of the truck, and one tire had blown. One of the teachers screamed at me at the top of his lungs, "Get back! It's going to blow!"

I yelled back, "It is if somebody doesn't do something!"

At this, the janitor took off. I turned one last time, and I screamed at the children, "Get your asses back now!"

Usually when an adult cusses at you as a kid, you would respond. At least that was my observation when I was a kid. There was no time for politeness, and they did back up a bit. They were still in harm's way; if it blew, somebody was going to get hurt. Then I spotted a mop leaned up against the fence. I grabbed it up, jabbed it in the hay, and as hard as I could, began to use one end to push the burning hay from one side and then the other. I was trying to move the burning hay from under the truck and the gas tank, so it did not explode.

I worked the mop side to side as quickly as I could. It was working. I was getting the hay out from under the truck. Finally, all the burning hay was on either side of the truck. The grass was already burned up under it, so it had nothing to burn. Luckily nothing on the truck was burning now. I pulled off my shirt and beat the hay. I slapped and stomped and fought it as fast as I could. Then all at once as quick as it had started, it was all over, and the fire was out. I could hear the fire truck in the distance, sirens blasting. I beat them to the draw, and it wouldn't be the last time. About that time, a janitor finally came running out with a fire extinguisher. I looked at him and said, "I could have used that about five minutes ago."

I rested against the fence. The sweat poured from me. I looked up to see a lady now standing close to the truck crying. I asked her if it was her truck. She replied that it was. She had won it from her husband in the divorce. It did not take me long to figure this one out.

The fireman came, and the teachers pointed at me and told the story. The chief came over, and I told him my part of the story. He asked me if I was all right, and I assured him I was okay. Then I walked back to my Ranger. I was about halfway there when I realized what I had just done. I started to shake, and chills ran up and down my body. I jumped in my truck and turned on the radio to hear "Midnight Rider" just starting to play. I cranked it up, let out a yell, and headed on to Mom and Dads.

I could not wait to tell the story. My brother was there, and we went back to see the truck being loaded onto a rollback. The next day, when I told the tale at work, they did not believe me. I told them to go to the school and ask anybody. The burn marks were in the grass as proof. One of the guys knew the janitor who had come late with the fire extinguisher. He called him, and he confirmed what had happened.

He said, "A man came out of nowhere driving a brand-new Ford Ranger. He came out of that truck and went to work on that fire. By the time I went to get a fire extinguisher and come back, he had it out. That truck could have easily at that point blew up. He didn't give any regard to himself. He was determined to get that fire out and protect those kids."

The next day, it was all over the plant. That afternoon, at the crowded time clock, my buddy Charley Tree yelled out, "Rick Ranger!"

The name stuck. Now, occasionally, I will tell that story, and I can still feel the heat and the chills. I have often wondered, "Do we have one great purpose?" Is there one great thing you were put here to do? Because of my experience fighting roaster fires, I was unafraid at the time. I am not comparing myself to the heroes around us every day. There are men and women who put it on the line for us daily. For me, though, it was my one great thing. I was in the right place at the right time and acted. If the good Lord put me on earth just for that, so be it. I will take that one thing and be proud of it. Only the people who know me when I pass away will know for sure.

I was known by all I worked with as Rick Ranger. Along the way, I would do things that bolstered my reputation. I became known as one of those people who would tackle anything. Later in my career, even when at different positions, I would be called in the middle of the night to fight roaster fires.

Once in the middle of the night, I was awakened to a phone call that the roasters were on fire, and they could not get them out. I grabbed my pants, put them on, and took off to the plant. When I reached the dock, smoke was billowing out of the bay doors. I ran back to the roasters to see ten people with fire extinguishers and a water hose trying in vain to put out the fire. They were from the spice room and the tea department. No one had a clue as to how to put out a roaster fire. They had not been trained to do so. I ran to the emergency spray stacks and pulled the levers. I then ran to the tool locker and grabbed an adjustable wrench and the asbestos gloves. I hollered for someone to get me a six-foot ladder. The roasters were burning good.

This one was a stack fire that had fallen from above and had caught both roasters on fire. I climbed on top of the roasters and went to work. I had by this time fought some good roaster fires but never with no shirt and no shoes. I got the bolts off, turned the pipes where I could get water to them, and started to put out the fire. I did this while the water poured from above, and the other roaster burned. I directed one of the mechanics to try to start taking off the wing nuts on the other roaster. Hot steam filled the air, and I tried to stay clear. Despite myself, I still received some burns and some singed hair. Once one of the roasters was out, I swung over by cable to the next, and soon it was out. I jumped down, turned on the exhaust fans to start clearing the smoke, and then shut the spray pipes off, which by this time had put thousands of gallons of water on the floor. You guessed it: everybody just looked at me, applauded, and said, "That's him. That's Rick Ranger right there."

Now about that time, the fire department showed up. I had a good head start on them. They came running in with axes drawn, ready to cut holes in the roof. I caught them as they were entering the roasting area. Stopping them, I told them, "It's all over, fellows. The fire is out. Don't go cutting any holes in the roof."

They looked at me sort of funny and started looking around to see if any fire was left.

I had told the mechanics to round up some wet vacuums to start cleaning up the mess. I then told the nighttime supervisor to put his people back to work. I said I was going to my locker to get a shirt and some shoes. About that time, the fire chief came rolling in and heading toward the roasters. I tried to stop him and tell him what was going on, but he pushed me aside and kept going. I thought, Okay, we will have to speak at some point, because nobody else knew what was going on.

I walked up front as more fire trucks were arriving. They had deployed three engine companies, I think. When a plant was on fire, I guess they knew to send enough folks to cover the job. I went to the plant phone covered in soot with wet black feet, called the then plant manager, and told him what was going on. I said, "There are three engine companies here, but I have the fire out now." I told him it was out before they got here. I then told him I did not know if we would be charged. They did not have to do anything. I said I would stay and clean up the mess.

I went to my locker and put on some old boots that I had in there with no socks. I found an old uniform shirt of mine in the dirty laundry basket and put it on. I went to the break room and fixed a pot of coffee. While it was brewing, I went downstairs and called my wife to tell her I was all right and to go to sleep. I would be a while. I went back up and poured myself a cup just as my name was being called on the intercom. It was one of the mechanics. He said that the fire chief wanted to talk to me. I told him, "You tell him I am upstairs having coffee. I need a break from firefighting. If he wants to talk to me, I am in the break room."

When he arrived up there, I said "I tried to tell you what happened downstairs."

He said, "You look different with a shirt and shoes on."

I just laughed and offered him a cup of coffee. As we sipped, I explained what had just happened, how it started, and how it was put out. It was then that he recognized me. He was the same chief from the elementary school fire.

He asked, "Do you make it a habit of running around putting out fires?"

I said, "No, I leave that kind of stuff to you guys. This time, it was my job to do it."

He was content with my answers and bid me good night. He said, "Next time, you might want to try it with a shirt and shoes on."

I raised my cup in acknowledgment. I drank it down and took another cup with me down to clean the mess.

When the plant manager arrived, I was still there that next morning. Before I left, I spoke to him and said that I thought it would be a good idea to train all the mechanics in roaster firefighting procedures. He agreed, and the next week, I wrote a standard operating procedure (SOP) and trained the mechanics from other departments in how to fight a roaster fire. So, the legend of Rick Ranger grew. What I had done with no shirt and no shoes went down in our plant's history and was told at many a lunch or coffee break. I enjoyed my little legend and tried always to live up to it. It wasn't always easy.

CHAPTER 13

THE FAMILY

Time went on by, and before you could remember it happening, four years had gone by. I was starting to wonder by this time if I was ever getting out of the coffee dump. I soon would be. I had been at this company for ten years. In that time, I had met some of the strangest characters. We had a variety of folks, like I said before, but now these people would be known to me as the family. Every occasionally, we would have a plant meeting. Sometimes they were good, sometimes bad. We either were being told about getting something new or raises or a change in benefits, which, for the first ten years or so, was almost always positive. In some cases, it was a plantwide butt-chewing. This meeting was a mix.

We were called together in the spice room, and all the equipment was shut down and air lines shut off. This was done to ensure complete quiet. We assembled and found places to lean or sit. Then Mr. Johnson came in, and he was, in a word, *mad*. The rest of us would soon find out that a whole bunch of sausage seasoning that we made for our meatpacking plant was done wrong. This had resulted in a whole lot of beef and pork being ruined. There had been a breakdown in the receiving of the product and the blending of the product, and the quality control checks somehow had let this get by. At the meatpacking plant, they had let it get by them as well, and it wound up in the stores. It was not in any way going to make anyone sick. It just made the product taste terrible. A recall was done, and butts were now being chewed.

He explained to us that manufacturing for this grocery chain was not set in stone. He told us how he had his job threatened by the head of all manufacturing about this mess up. What I was now hearing for the first time in my time there was the phrase: "They might shut us down!" We were told that it was a constant fight for the manufacturing plants to stay alive. Then it was further said we did not need to give them a reason to rid themselves of the headaches that came with manufacturing their own products. He then said it was possible that they might ask us to quit producing some of our products, followed by that if he had to let people go, the sorry ones were going first. He then said, "You know who you are. You are the ones among you who don't really care about your jobs. You are the ones who drag in late and don't mind missing time and putting the load on your coworkers. You will be first."

People looked around the room from one to another.

He then said, "I want you all to look around the room! These people in this room are your family!" His voice lifted, and he added, "These are your brothers and your sisters. You all have always pulled together. It does not matter about your race, your religion, or your status in this company, from us in the front office to the lowest paid one here. I have seen when one of you are sick or had a crisis in your lives that the group as a whole lifts that family member up. It is time now to pull together and don't let your brother or sister down. Keep your eyes on your family. Don't take an it's-the-other-person's-responsibility attitude. What happens in this plant affects you all." He finished by saying, "Overall, you are a great, hardworking group of people. Stick together, and keep your eye on the ball." With that, he left the room, and we all went back to our respective jobs.

Mr. Johnson was a great leader and was as good at giving a speech as anybody I ever heard. He took what was a butt-chewing and flipped it around in the middle of the speech to make us feel better about ourselves. He had a way of doing that at times. This, however, was one of the better ones. The people in the plant were a family, at least at that time. If someone was in the hospital, you could count on numerous visits, cards, and flowers from the company and the workers. If you were out for very long, a couple of weeks or so, someone would always pass the hat. We collected money to help them get by. Sometimes groceries were bought, and chores that they could not do were taken care of. If a new baby came along, we celebrated, and if someone passed away, we all mourned and did what we could for the family. If a close family member of someone at the plant, say a mother or father, passed away, the plant was shut down for anyone to attend. If it was an employee, we all went.

In today's world, we are lucky to even get the time off, period. The working world has become hard on this issue. It would be unthinkable today for a plant to shut down and lose profit for one day.

It is thought of now as an intrusion of someone's rights to pass the hat to help a coworker. People who are now indifferent to the other guy's plight feel as if it is solicitation in the workplace. The world has sadly become all about me, what can I get, and how can I get my share of the other guy's pie? The more things tighten down, the more we see this perspective. I sure hate John's out sick, but this will help me because the time he is missing I am gaining ground. They might get rid of him, and that will help secure my spot, or I can get his. I hate that John's dad passed away, but I'd rather show the boss that I'd rather be here working for the company than go to the funeral and show John some respect.

I don't like to write these things about our working world now, but you all know it is true. If it wasn't for the misfortune of someone at times, there would be nowhere in some companies to go. There are not even jobs to go to. How many people do you know look at the obituaries to see if someone has passed away and where they were employed? Where I worked for a long time, we were family.

The family was broken down into different groups. You had the office bunch. This consisted of three secretaries, one for the plant manager, one for the assistant plant manager, and one who assisted the buyer and was responsible for inventory. You had an HR manager who handled all employee benefit issues and policy problems. There were the girls in the lab. These were for the most part a normal group.

Then you had the tea department. This was mostly now a group of older gals, many of whom I had worked with when I was in the tea department. You had a mechanic who now sort of ran the department and was a supervisor to boot. He told many a tall tale and was known for doing just that. His nickname was Nam. He, according to him, flew helicopters in the Vietnam War and had made many a daring mission. He hunted raccoons with the old supervisor, and that was how he came to be where he was. He was a whiz though with the tea machines. The other supervisor, whom they called "the Fortunate One," had at least six of his family members working at the plant in one place or another. They called him fortunate because he was kicked in the head by a horse and survived. Then, there was my tea blending buddy and his night-shift counterpart. The other guy was a poor fellow who for a month or so would read the Bible and at other times worship the devil. He, knowing I could draw, asked me once to come to his house and draw a pentagram on his wall. Though he told me he would give me one hundred dollars to do so, I declined. He had some serious issues.

Then there was one supervisor whose brother was a big shot at headquarters. He was a fine and generous man with a good nature about him. He worked with three guys. The first was one we called "Poor Devil." He was about 120 pounds soaking wet. He was another nice guy, but when he got to drinking, he was ten foot tall and bullet-proof. He had gone on a deep-sea fishing trip with some of the other guys. He became drunk aboard ship and made quite a few folks angry. When they arrived back at the dock, a huge fight broke out, and several of the guys had to get involved. The outcome was not pretty with busted lips and black eyes all around.

There was Steven, a quiet redneck and, at that time, one of the biggest guys in the plant. He spoke slowly, deliberately, and meant what he said. He went about his business quietly. Then there was Joey. Joey was, in one word, *different*. Joey would do whatever he could to shock everybody. He changed hairstyles as often as some people change their socks. A Mohawk one day, the next week bright blue, the next week white, and then shaved—you just never knew what to expect from Joey. He was a strange one. But he was as good a forklift driver as we had.

There was the spice room group, which was a mix of elderly women from different ethnic backgrounds. We had some black ladies, some white ladies, some brown ladies, and this very tiny Filipina lady. She was so small they had to build her a stand to get up on to pack spices. Big Ben was the supervisor, and a nicer person you would be hard pressed to find. You had Russ, the mechanic who was always funny. You had Rusty the spice room operator who was a sincere, soulful guy. We had another mechanic there they called Callahan, who could smoke a cigarette, dip snuff, and chew on a toothpick while he drank coffee. He was a multitalented guy.

Then there was Mr. Nut, a crazy-acting fellow who really was a good man. He was from the farm country of Georgia, spoke with a deep accent, and carried himself as such. Slow Joe was very slow minded. He would get upset at little things and would openly cry.

Then, the mill room guys—there was Mr. Tool, Jim, Fred, and my pal B. Now Mr. Tool and Jim were old salts from the navy. Both had fought the Japanese in the Pacific. They were good men, and Jim was somewhat of a philosopher. Both were tough guys. Fred was a new guy, and just about everything Fred said was a fabrication of some sort. B. was a hardworking black dude who could get along in any crowd and was well liked. We have been friends now for over thirty years. He started about when I did.

There was then the receiving crew. They were known as the Rat Patrol. You had Jim, the hard-nose supervisor. Then you had his back-up P. Boy, Charlie Tree, and Lurch. Then, there were Mr. Wonderful, who was so called because of his softball skill, and the Hawk, a huge brother with twenty-two-inch biceps and as soft a heart as you've ever seen. Over time, the characters changed, and different ones would take their places in our family.

Then there was my group, the Coffee Boys. You had Happy, who had gone to coffee just before I did, and Tomcat, the supervisor, who was, as the name applies, just that. He was known for it in our community outside the plant as well. Bubba was the mechanic who could fix anything but was not about to work on anything unless it was down. He spent his days, if the line was running, looking out the dock and chewing Red Man. You had Dewayne, the packer, and the Lizard, who was another packer. This would change for both these guys; both were hard workers and good with tools. There was the Whip and then me.

Then, there was the sanitation crew, one of whom was Slick Willie. Willie, although he had the lowest-paying job in the plant as janitor, dressed better than anybody in the place. Willie, daily, wore a three-piece suit to work. He played the dogs a lot, and Willie could not drive a car. He was always good about giving money for any cause. He was always good humored.

Then there was the Who Ha clan. They were three Filipino guys who cleaned like madmen. They gambled a lot as well and always had more cash money than anyone, save Mr. Johnson, in the plant.

Over the course of many years, we had a very wide variety of folks. We had two convicted murders and one who was charged with murder. The first one was a fellow I could not have imagined would hurt anybody. Old Jess was a black dude who shook a lot when he wasn't drinking, but he always seemed harmless in any situation. They said he had shot and killed a man who had beaten his sister. Old Jess was later acquitted when his sister came forward and admitted she had been the one to pull the trigger. Even though Old Jess had gone to jail, he fell right back in with the family when he was released.

The next was a guy we called "the Hurricane." He was so named for two reasons. One was he rode a motorcycle that was named Hurricane, and the other was his temper, which was like a storm. He would fly off the handle and challenge anybody to a fight over nothing. When news came that he was arrested for killing a drug dealer that his brother had been in a fight with, it did not surprise me. Then after he was convicted and put into prison; it did not surprise me when he wound up dead in his cell. He had been an Army Ranger, and it was a sad way for him to end up.

The third though was a crafty fellow named Amp. Now he befriended as many people at the plant as he could and tried to fit right on in. I figure myself to always be a good judge of character, and in this case, I was right. I knew there was something distrustful about him. I, on several occasions, had noticed that he would be walking across the parking lot well after time to be at work. I observed this a few times, and one day, at the time clock, I saw Mr. Nut punching his timecard. This reminded me once again of the hardware situation.

I pulled Mr. Nut to the side and said, "Don't do that, Mr. Nut; they will fire you for doing that."

He replied, "Amp just called on the wall phone and said he would be here in a minute and asked if I would punch his card." He continued, "I didn't see the harm in it."

I then asked, "How many times has Amp asked you to do this?"

He answered, "I don't know, four times maybe."

I asked, "Has it just been in the morning?"

He said, "No, the other day, he told me he would be late coming back for lunch and asked if I would do it then."

"How late was he?" I continued with my questioning.

He said, "About an hour or so."

I told Mr. Nut, "Don't ever do it again. He is going to get you fired." I then told him to let Amp solve his own problems.

The next week, the police showed up at work and arrested Amp. The day Mr. Nut had covered for him by punching his timecard for lunch, Amp had robbed a local liquor store. He shot the clerk in the face, killing him. He took the money and the gun home and hid them along with a mask. Then he came back to work as if nothing had happened. According to the timecard, if Mr. Nut kept his mouth shut, he had an alibi. What he did not count on was his accomplice turning himself in and turning over Amp. They found the mask, the gun, and a small amount of cash under his bed at home. Mr. Nut told them about the timecards. Amp is now on death row.

CHAPTER 14

BRICK PACK

Not long after the sausage seasoning incident, something happened. Mr. Johnson gathered us coffee boys together. He then announced that to keep up with the current trend of the coffee business, we were buying a brick pack machine. It would increase shelf life, and the coffee would be fresher. The drawback for now was to keep up with current production, we would have to go to two shifts. This would be done until the following year when we could buy another machine. They were a quarter of a million dollars apiece, and we could only afford one at a time. This would have no immediate effect on the roasting area. There was a degassing process to solve but not until later. Mr. Johnson knew how to run a manufacturing plant. He knew that old equipment, when it became outdated and could not keep up to industry standards, needed to be replaced. He, in many cases, had updated equipment and brought in new lines to run in his tenure. He never had a problem getting money from our parent company to do so.

The next day, he came back to the dump. He asked me if I would be interested in learning to run the new brick pack machine when it came in. I jumped at the chance. I assured him I would love to. He said it would be a month before it was up and running. In the meantime, he would look for me a replacement for the coffee dump. I was very happy, to say the least. I knew it meant a swing shift, but I also knew it meant a dollar an hour raise. Soon Fred came from the mill room, and I was set about training him for my job and how to roast. He had set his eyes on being the roaster.

Now as I settled into learning the machine, I had worked out a deal with Happy: I would take all nights. I did this because my then wife worked nights, and I could be on the same schedule. This gave me a chance to learn things about the machine with no one watching over my shoulder. It was a prototype from Italy. It had computer controls and robotic parts. It was the neatest thing in the plant. I learned the ins and outs and then set about figuring out how to make it run just a little better. I found that when it was running well, after an hour or so, you could increase the line speed. This would not happen all the time though. You had to know when to pull back and let it settle into a rhythm. We shut down early every night so Dewayne and the Lizard could clean up, and I would then do the paperwork.

The Lizard was so named because he could climb anything with just his arms. He drove a lime-green truck as well. Dewayne was a tall, lanky fellow, quick and very smart. Almost every night, we produced more coffee than the day shift.

Part of this was because of what I had learned about the machine, and the other part was that Happy could not keep his hands off it. He couldn't help himself; he was constantly tinkering with it, trying to get it to look just a little better. He kept shutting down the line, and it could never get in a steady rhythm. I had learned not to shut the line down unless I just had to. I had learned that by adjusting the variables on the vacuum chambers through the computer, I could enhance the way the bags looked. This way, I would not have to make manual adjustments like Happy was doing. I was beating his production and running thirty minutes less a night. Nobody could figure it out, and that included Bubba. I tried over and over to tell him to simply leave it alone, but he could not. He just had to use those wrenches.

Now something else too: I was teaching both of my guys to run the line. This way, if the line went down and I was in the bathroom, one of them could clear it and restart it. Happy insisted nobody touch that line but him.

We became known as the A team. My two pals and I worked like clockwork together and always did a good job. Now off work, we became great friends. We hunted and fished together. We rode the woods and the creeks and had one adventure after the next. Many times on Friday night, we would put a case of beer on ice at lunch. We would go down the road to this old company parking lot after our shift and drink beer until morning.

On many occasions, our other associates joined in the fun and the storytelling. It was great fun unless we stayed out too much past daylight and would get in trouble with the wives.

This went on for a great while, the whole year. When the next machine was delayed coming in from Italy, it meant we would stay on nights longer. The other guys' wives worked days, and something had to give. Mine had just moved to a swing shift, so I approached the Tomcat and said we would like to rotate. "We have worked nights for over a year, and the boys want to be home with their wives." So, we worked out a rotation, and it took the Italians another four months to get the machine to us. When it was finally up and running, I was asked about another position. It had become essential to build new holding tanks for the coffee lines because of the degassing problem. The coffee needed to sit for twenty-four hours after it was ground before packaging. Someone needed to learn the new system and be responsible for the grinding. I was asked to do it and the coffee quality control as well.

A lab was built for me to work in and doubled as my office. This job was a breeze compared to what I had been doing. I enjoyed this job, and it was going to be a natural transition to supervisor.

Dewayne moved to relief operator and eventually mechanic. The Lizard was asked to go to the new gravy department. He was made a mechanic there and flourished at it. He turned out to be good at fixing the new machines. He hated to leave us. We, at that time, had called it "the dark side." It was a newly formed department. Mr. Johnson saw the profit in gravy mixes and had acquired the space from the parent company's drug warehouse. New rooms were built, new machines were bought, and a whole new crew was hired to outfit it.

Now the Lizard, who did not mind working, always said though, "I would rather be dead than work my whole life."

One Saturday night, he realized that dream when his lottery numbers were called, and the Lizard received ten million dollars. As far as I know, he has not worked since, and a nicer guy it couldn't have happened to.

CHAPTER 15

ENTER CY CHUNG

As we grew and different departments were added, it became obvious we needed a full-time sanitation technician, someone who knew industry standards and pesticides that were safe for use in food environments. A Chinese fellow was hired and brought in to clean the place up and organize quality control. An outside inspection company that monitored all the manufacturing plants had begun auditing us. These people left no stone unturned and were very thorough. Their scores meant everything. We were now being held to industry standards.

Cy went about sealing every crack and crevice so no type of infestation could occur. He had degrees in food safety and in every phase of the process along the way. It was not long before three of the Who Ha Clan decided it was time to retire. Only one, who had been certified with different chemicals for spraying and fogging, remained. Cy was quickly fixing our problems with moths, rodents, and insects, period.

Once in quality control, he purchased new testing equipment. We had what was known as a color meter. Before we just had an old sample of what the coffee was supposed to look like, and if it matched, we let the roast go. Now, with the color meter, we could be exact as to what the color was. A new standard of pulling roast checks and documenting them every thirty minutes was established.

Now, one day, Whip had begun roasting. The new grinding system could outrun the roasters with ease. With one statement from Happy, the Whip went berserk. Happy said to him, "Rick is going to run you down with those new grinders. He will have to shut them down, and you know what that will mean."

The Whip shook his fist at Happy, and when he saw me firing up the grinders, he shook his fist at me. I did not know what for.

When Happy told me what he had said to him, I told him that they wouldn't do anything because they knew the grinders were faster than the roasters.

Happy said with a grin, "I know that, but the Whip doesn't. Serves him right all the years he hung running out over somebody's head."

I just shrugged it off. I had things to do.

As he was roasting, I pulled a sample, and it was still in range but on the dark side. I told him it was heading out of range and to go down in temperature or back off the gas. I then documented it and went to break. He must have thought it was some kind of trick to outrun him, so he went up on the gas to make the roasters run faster. The following roast was burned up. He knew it was burned but decided to let it go. Pulling it out of the cooler would cost him more time. Instead, he tried to hurry it up before being caught. The golden rule of roasting was never, ever to send up a burned roast.

Just then, Cy showed up to make a random check. He went straight to what was left of the burned roast, pulled a sample, went to the lab, and saw it was burned up. He got the Tomcat and instructed him to shut down the roasters. He then took the sample and my documentation that I had just made instructing the Whip to go down on the next roast. He went straight to Mr. Johnson. If he had not sent it up, it would have been okay. Once it was up in the bins, it was too late to do anything about it. The problem was we had been getting some complaints about burned coffee already. Mr. Johnson wondered how many had he sent up burned before and hid it. Mr. Johnson called the Tomcat to the office and told him to send the Whip home. He wanted me on the roasters that day and from then on until we could trust Fred.

They sent the Whip home, and he was one of these guys that you might see on TV for going on a shooting rampage. He had threatened to do so on many occasions.

When the day was through, I went to Mr. Johnson and asked that they give him another chance. I told him I would monitor him and would look out after him. Mr. Johnson said to me, "I appreciate what you're trying to do, but I can't trust him anymore, and you can't be babysitting the highest-paid blue-collar job in the plant. The coffee business is too tight, and we can't lose our customers to burnt roasts."

I then asked, "You're not going to fire him, are you?"

He looked at me, and I could tell he was thinking about it.

I reasoned, "Mr. Johnson, you know he has never been quite right. I can see demoting him, but to fire him just wouldn't be right. He can't help how he is."

He said, "I don't know what I am going to do with him."

I said, "Okay, that's all I had to say. I will be on the roasters in the morning."

Before I left, he stopped me and asked, "Rick, after the torment he put you through back there, why would you come in here and defend him?"

I said, "Two reasons, number one, I thought it was the right thing for me to do."

He asked, "And the second?"

I looked at him real hard and said, "He's less apt to want to kill all of us if he still has a job."

He half smiled and nodded his head at me, and with that, I left. Nobody ever told the Whip I went in there and pleaded for his job. The Whip still hated me.

Well, they demoted the Whip and moved him to a packer position. When he realized it was me who was moved to take his place, his hatred for me just embedded forever. I did not want his place; I was enjoying the job I had. I was within a quarter an hour of the roaster's pay, and I was not tied down to the roasters.

Fred, being the kind of guy who loved to stir things up, decided to pick at the Whip. When he would see him on the line, he would walk by and just laugh. The anger would rise in the Whip.

One day, about two weeks after he had been demoted, Fred went to the Whip. He then demanded the Whip give him his key to the tool cabinet for the roasters. When the Whip refused, he looked at him and said, "You might as well give it to me. They will never let you back around those roasters again."

With that, the Whip picked up one of the brick pack coffee bags and cracked Fred right upside the head. Fred retreated to the coffee dump with a small cut and a knot on his head. Fred could have taken him to the office, but for some reason, he let it go. Maybe it was the same reason I had defended him to Mr. Johnson. The Whip retired within a year.

So, as it was, I roasted and took care of the grinding system both. I did have quality control to do my checks. I settled in, and for two more years, I roasted. Same old grind, you could say, pun intended.

Hot summers and mild winters were the norm for Florida. In the summer, it would be 130 degrees Fahrenheit in front of the roasters. That was with a big industrial fan blowing straight at you. It was good and hot for sure. Winters were nice except for the orders picked up, and the days would be long. Many times, you went in while it was still dark and left at dark. Other than looking out the ceiling fan hole or a dock door, you might never see the sun.

I bought a house. I settled into my life. People came into our company family and left. Some passed away; others retired. We saw new faces come and go. Some you could tell wanted a job, and others did not. I only knew of one firing at that time.

This had occurred at the detergent plant that was tied into our plant. We shared the same building, but they were their own entity. They made laundry soap and that sort of thing for our parent company. They had a tower for making the detergent, and it was a good forty feet off the ground. One night, this one guy who was working his way through college decided to have some fun. He rode the elevator to the top and took an old blue-ink bottle with him. He had filled the gallon jug with water to see what would happen if you dropped it from forty feet. I don't know what he majored in, but obviously common sense wasn't it.

Down below was a white company truck and some brand-new equipment. He dropped the gallon jug, and it exploded into a blue bomb of blue ink. He just filled that jug with water. The permanent ink left in the bottle was enough to coat truck and the equipment. They ran a hose to it, but to no avail, the ink was there to stay. The truck and equipment would have to be painted. He was terminated.

CHAPTER 16

THE END OF
THE BREAD

One day, I went home to hear a message on my answering machine from my mom that I needed to call Dad. I did, and I found out they were making plans to close the bakery. My father had put forty years into the bakery and was one year and a half from retirement. He was devastated. He had been the second one ever hired for the bakery after it was built. It was his life; he was there more than he was home. He knew the place better than anybody.

What had happened was that it had not been updated to keep up with current industry production. Plant managers were given bonuses to keep costs down and maximize profit. Many times, my father had said that his manager would pocket larger bonuses rather than get new equipment. He also said that the manager was using cheaper and cheaper ingredients. This caused the bread to go stale faster. This caused sales to go down. This eventually caused the parent company to research the bakery harder. When they did, their study found that the bakery was outdated. It would cost millions by this time to renovate it. Had it been done along the way, this would not have happened, at least not yet.

So, it came time to figure out what to do with my dad. Some of the other guys were able to transfer to other plants. We received a few at our plant. My dad would not be so lucky. Because of his age, they only offered to let him to go ahead and retire. He had asked if he could just go and sweep floors or anything until his true retirement age. They refused and told him that the only jobs left were the ones unloading trucks. At the age of sixty-one and a half, that wasn't going to happen. He had given them everything he had in him. And he was now being let go.

When the time came, however, to close the place, they did let him make as much time as he could. He assisted in preparing the equipment for sale. He helped ship out the last of the product. He then went about cleaning each area for the new owners of whatever was next.

Once all the equipment and materials were gone, my dad locked the bay doors, locked the office, locked the front gate, and took the keys to headquarters. He came home and was never the same. It had hurt him so badly; it was a wound that was not going to heal.

My father, if cut, would have bled the company blood. Now he was bitter. Why after hearing the employees for years ask for new equipment did nobody do anything? Why had nobody stepped in from upper management? People over the plant manager had to know this was going on. Why did the quality control folks do nothing when they realized that the cheap ingredients were killing the product? Why was there no place he could make his time?

These questions burned holes in him. Had it not been that my cousin and I still worked for the company, he would never have bought groceries from them again. It was true: he had made a good living there for forty years, and he had a very good retirement account. That was not it to him. He wanted to see the bakery go on. He wanted to see it thriving and competing with the other bakeries that made bread for the parent company. He wanted to walk out of that door seeing the place as good as or better than it was when it opened. He wanted for years to complete his time there. It was a matter of pride, not money. This concept is totally and utterly unheard of today.

His bitterness toward them was causing me trouble. I could not stand to hear him talk about my company that way. I knew what happened was wrong. Nobody had listened to him, and he could not make them change things. I reasoned that my plant was different. My plant manager made improvements all along the way so far. We were still competing on a high level. I had now been with them approaching fifteen years. I was as company as he had been. I believed in what we were doing and stood behind it.

One Sunday after dinner, as we watched football, we began to discuss the company. I really did not want to because I now felt different than he did about it. It started because a commercial came on for the company, and dad couldn't let it go.

He said, "Well, there they go again, trying to make you love them."

I replied, "Dad, let's not talk about it. We don't have the same opinions on them anymore."

He said, "Now they got you brainwashed too."

"No, I am not," I replied.

He said, "Better not wait all your life to realize some things. The company is changing and not for the better when it comes to the employees. You are becoming just a number to them."

I reasoned, "Look, don't judge the company by what your plant manager did. He did not do the things he should have to keep you in business."

He told me this. "The face of manufacturing is changing. The chain you are working for is changing. The old guard are dying out or leaving. The way the blue-collar man is being looked at has changed. You are a number on a timecard that must be paid and insured. You are a name by a matrix that shows your abilities and faults and the time you have missed and what your weaknesses may be. You have no face, no soul to the company. It is all business now. There is no room for compassion in the workplace. Your fate will always lie in not what you do, but what men sitting around a table with larger profits on their mind want."

I did not want to hear it. I did not want to believe that. I wanted to think that what I did mattered. I thought, Well, maybe in a boardroom, yes, they don't care, but they do at the plant.

I felt like we all mattered. He was right that the old-timers who ran the company were leaving and retiring. They were rich and had done well. They had given back quite a bit to the city in which the business started.

I had heard this before, that the old-timers cared more about the employees. The reason was they started the company as employees.

They did not graduate out of college to go into the working world. They started out in the working world and had made the company with hard work and sweat. They realized the struggles of blue-collar folks because they were blue-collar folks. Now, what Dad was trying to say was the people who were starting to run the companies were coming out of colleges. The way they looked at it was this was business; there was no room for sentimental feelings. You cannot make changes for more profit if you let your conscience get in the way. The goal is not the betterment of the employee but the profit margin of the company. Big profits meant a more stable company.

I did not want to accept that reality. It was sort of like being told that your spouse is cheating on you, and you don't want to believe it. So, you don't. You reason that they couldn't hurt you that way, and you lie to yourself. You try to convince yourself that there must be some kind of mistake. I think they call it denial. I was so convinced I could make a difference I was willing to doubt my dad, who until this point had never led me astray. I was willing to reason to myself that perhaps it was just business. The bakery was dragging the company down. If they did not cut it loose, we would all be dragged down with it. They had found jobs for most of the guys in the company. A lot of the guys who were there with Dad just retired. Dad would be okay. He was just bitter.

Dad tried to stay home and could not. He had to get out and do something. My mom was about seven years younger than my dad, so she was nowhere near retirement. Staying at home was driving him crazy. He had lost his identity. He was at the bakery, and now it was gone. He did not know what to do with himself. There was another thing to realize: my dad's brothers had all passed away. Almost all of them had died in their early sixties. My dad had already suffered a heart attack, and they did not know as much about the heart then. So doing something very physical was out.

After some time, he became a security guard. I remembered it worried us all so much because he took a job at a bank. He was responsible for going in with one of the tellers to open the place up early. He would not carry a gun. He said that would just give someone the excuse to shoot him.

He continued to do that job for over a year. It gave him something to do. He began to like the job, and they liked him. He would open the bank and make coffee for all the workers there. He was well liked by the bank manager, and he only worked about four or five hours a day. I would go and eat lunch with him every chance I got. He would pop up at my house on Saturday mornings, and we would drink coffee. After a while, we did not talk much about the company anymore. Then one day, as I was about to head out of town for vacation, Momma called and said Dad had passed away.

My brother was out of town celebrating his fortieth birthday. It was my job to break the news to him and get him home. He was very close to my father, as we all were. He was loved by our family. My younger brother was in shock, and Mom was inconsolable. I put my grief off for later and soldiered on to be the rock for the family. My dad had told me on many occasions when this time came, I would be the one. I would have to be strong for the family and be there from then on for my mom.

My older brother took it hard, and my younger brother, who has always had such a soft heart, was devastated. My dad, in his wisdom, knew this would be the case. I made the arrangements that were not already done. I stayed by my mom's side steadfast.

My aunt told me to let it out, not to try to be strong. I told her I could not. It was my father's wish that I remain calm, do my job, and get us through this. I could not break down. The family had to know there was one of us that no one needed to worry about. That meant our extended family too. Dad had touched so many young men's lives by being a role model to them they were like his other sons. They grieved for him as if he were their father. It hurt for them as it did us. She said to me, "If you do not let it out of you now, your father's passing will stay with you for a very long time." She was right, as that has been over fifteen years ago, and I welled up with emotion as I wrote this.

This part, I dedicate to my father, Doyle A. Johnson.

CHAPTER 17

CARRYING ON

Times were getting tough for me now. I tried to get back into the swing of things. I went back to roasting coffee and dealing with the day-to-day things. Finally, Fred moved into roasting, and I went back to the grinder operator and started working closer with the quality control department. My marriage began to take on water soon after my father passed. Time and circumstances had let us drift apart, and within three months, we were divorced. When this happened, I thought it was the worst thing that could happen to me. This, as it turned out, was a blessing to me.

It came to pass that Mr. Johnson retired. He went on to be a tea broker and left the plant behind. It was time. He was sixty-some-odd years old. When this happened, I lost my best supporter. He believed in me and what I could do more than anybody else. He would never have let me down. The next plant manager did not feel the same about me. He was a good man and had a good heart. I think he thought I was too bold and a little too honest in my opinions.

Fred, however, had managed to smooth his way into the new plant manager's confidence. What the new plant manager would find out the hard way was Fred was full of bull. Fred had managed to get the new plant manager onto the golf course with him. He cuddled up close and weaved him a bunch of stories and funny anecdotes. Fred was closing in on something. I could not figure out what.

What I knew about Fred that the plant manager did not was his work ethic stank. He was out sick and consistently late and would cop an attitude and slow down on his work. The reason he did not know was the Tomcat had let him slide repeatedly. He never dragged Fred on the carpet, so there was no paper trail to prove anything. You could, however, have pulled timecards and sick leave notices to see what he had been up to.

Then it came to light that there were going to be some changes in the office. The buyer was going to leave, as well, because of his age. This was a suit-and-tie job, and the pay was considerably higher than that of the floor jobs. When the plant found out that this was happening and someone from the floor would be promoted, they thought it would be me. I did not know whom they wanted. It had been hinted to me by the new plant manager once. He had mentioned there might be other jobs other than the floor I might be considered for. He said this to me when he was the assistant plant manager. Then I thought, Why not me? I have put in my time so I could do that job. I was good enough at ordering supplies for our department that I could order for the plant. I thought, Yeah, why not me?

When they announced it would be Fred, my heart sank. I had ten years' seniority on him and the hard work behind me to show what I had done. Now they were giving this guy an office job for doing nothing more than playing golf with the boss. The Tomcat came to me and apologized. He asked me not to feel hard at him. I did though because when given the chance, he did not speak up about Fred. He had kept me there for his benefit. He needed me to run that department for him. This would not be the last time he would hold me back.

I felt betrayed. It was the first time since I had been there that a promotion was there to get, and I did not get it. It really hurt. The plant manager was friends with the Tomcat, and he was protecting him using me. When the new machines and equipment came in, the Tomcat became incapable of knowing how to operate them and could not figure out timetables for them. He did not know how to order for them or how much to put in the system to get the orders he needed. I had been doing it for years for him.

The plant joined in my dismay and disbelief. The family knew about Fred and what he really was. They were held down on policy and watched Fred skate by. The plant did not receive this well. It showed that it did not matter what you did if you kissed up to the boss. Hard work and playing by the rules would not get you ahead as quickly as a few rounds of golf.

I could not contain myself, and I openly expressed my anger over this situation. I let the people of the plant know I thought it was wrong. Many of the family came to me and ranted that the job should have been mine. I could see what I had learned at the hardware store. I wasn't realizing the fruits of my labor. The Tomcat was eating my fruit and collecting a fat salary doing it. There was nothing I could do about it. I was making good money and had a growing retirement account. So, I waited.

As Fred tried to settle into his job, his flaws started becoming obvious. He was screwing up royally. He had botched order after order, and though I knew it was hurting the plant, I took solace in it. The inventory was becoming unmanageable, and production orders were being shorted for lack of supplies. He was showing up late and missing time. He openly flirted with the girls in the office. He was as unprofessional as he could be.

Then, one day, the plant manager came in to find Fred lying on his private secretary's desk. He was sprawled out talking to her. I would not have believed this had I not seen it with my own eyes. I had gone into the office to copy a blend sheet, and there he was. Just at that moment, the plant manager walked in. The look in his eyes when he saw what Fred was doing was another one of those priceless moments.

He yelled, "Fred, get off that damn desk, and come into my office!"

Fred was demoted to the rat patrol. He had embarrassed the plant manager enough.

That was the beginning of the end for our plant manager. He had put his secretary in the buyer's position. And she would need my help to order materials. I had always thought she was a sweet, good-hearted person. So, when orders came for our department, I knew the formulas to get the materials to fill them and the lead time our material suppliers would need. So, I helped as much as I could.

Now a whole chain of events began to unfold. Callahan, who was a mechanic, had been put in charge of the new gravy rooms. He knew more about the machines, as he had helped put them in. He had brought in a pal of his he grew up with. His name was Jeep. It came to pass that the mechanics' supervisor retired. The superintendent who hired me passed away. The shipping supervisor retired, and they shut down the bag plant next door to us all in about eighteen months. Callahan up and quit to help his pa-in-law in the air-conditioning business. What happened next once again angered me to no end.

It was mandated by our parent company that women and minorities were to get the next management positions. So Big Ben became the superintendent, which he deserved. He was not a minority, but he had been there longer and knew more about the plant than anybody. He did not know as much about coffee as me only because that was the one department he had not really worked in.

Jeep, not a minority, went to head of the mechanics and was made their supervisor. He had just started there, yet he made friends with the plant manager fast—and you get the picture. Bubba thought he should have been awarded the position. After all, he was able to keep the machines running so well he could hang out by the dock door two hours a day. He quit. Two of the girls who were packers and didn't have a clue about running a department were made supervisors because of the mandate from headquarters. One took Callahan's place; the other took the spice room where Big Ben had been. Then they promoted P Boy to shipping supervisor. His dad was the mechanics supervisor who had just retired. He was not the first choice, though. My pal Charlie Tree was, but he refused the job. Tree was smart and capable. P Boy knew the job. It was not offered to Fred, and he quit. Then the Fortunate One, who ran the tea department at night, retired, and Charlie Tree once again was offered that position. He refused, and because they needed someone black, the Hawk was given the position.

Let me get something straight before I go on. I have never, ever had any reservations about a minority being promoted if they earned it. I have always been and continue to be an advocate that the best person for the job should have it. In that way, the company is stronger because the best talent you have is being used.

If you had a football team that competed for money, would you play your best players or play team members because of their gender or color. The idea is to run a strong company. These people who were promoted were family to me, and I care about each one. You could use the word *love*. I continue to this day to have relationships with these folks. This is not malice toward them but a reflection of what I went through. The reality of the situation was it led to the eroding of morale and weakened the plant. I understand the concept that minorities and women did not for a long time play on a level playing field. Leveling the field is one thing. To reward a person without merit is wrong, though.

I was pulled into the office one day, and it was explained to me that the plant manager's hands were tied, and he did what he had to do. That did not help the fact that I was being once again passed over. I was told the Tomcat wouldn't be around much longer so I should just do my job and keep my nose clean. I was promised that position when it came available. It was the same story: I was kept where I could babysit him, and that was it. I knew it, the plant knew it, and instead of justice being served for me, it was not. I was disgruntled at first. Then I became quiet. I drew into myself and spoke very little or at all to anyone. This went on for a couple of months. I was not angry with the family; I was just mulling my position.

The quiet was unnerving to my supervisor and to the family. I was one of the best players on the team, if not the best. The family became afraid I might leave. This was on my mind because I had an offer to go to another coffee plant. It was our rival I had competed against all this time. Whether to start over was the question. Once again, not many choices here, either put up with the current situation or quit.

After a long time, I concluded that it was still better that I stay. I had three weeks' worth of vacation, and I was getting a good salary. I still had the offer of the other coffee plant out there. I had a friend who worked there who assured me he could get me on with all my coffee experience. Although the lure was there and I felt that I had been passed over, I did not want to start at the bottom again. I was now at twenty years of service. They were playing a card that I realized they were playing. They knew that I cared. They knew that I cared more about that plant than myself. They knew I was not the kind of person to just give up. I had been taking quite a beating at their hands. I spent many sleepless nights wondering what I had done to have not been awarded what I wanted all this time. I have wanted that white shirt ever since I started there.

One day the human resource manager was walking by and stopped to talk to me. He said, "Rick, can I talk to you for a minute?"

I said, "Sure, what do you need?"

He said, "It's about what I have seen happening with you." He continued, "I know you are frustrated and upset about what has happened here."

I replied, "Yeah, I am. I feel kind of beat down."

He then asked, "Why don't you go and get your bachelor's degree?"

I asked, "Why? What good does the degree do for me here?"

He then went on, "The good old boy promotions and stuff that have been going on around here will not last much longer. The man with the degree will get the promotions. The winds are changing. You have the brains to do it. Just go and do it now before you are any older."

I thought about it for a while and then reasoned that I would not need a degree to go to the next level. The Tomcat's job would be mine if I held on. That was a decision I should have considered more carefully. It would haunt me later but not just yet.

I turned back up the intensity level and put my mind back to my work. I had convinced myself I was not just doing it for me but for the family. I was a team player, and I would not ever be accused of not doing all I could for the plant to keep it strong and going forward. I would fight right on for them, and at the very least, I would have that honor, which could not be taken away from me. I still gave it my all, and I would be satisfied with doing that. Now, though the winds that the human resource manager warned about were beginning to blow, what I did not know was I was fixing to get a tail wind to help me along.

CHAPTER 18

THE LEAN MEXICAN

There came a day when all the plants underwent a change. Enter the California Boys and the beginning of *lean manufacturing*. This concept came from Japan—or so we were told—and is a very efficient way to eliminate waste in all its forms. It can come as wasted materials, time, or flesh. Mostly flesh. The idea is simple: when they say lean, they mean the workforce. The concept was the same as always: maximize profits for the owners and maybe the stockholders too. Each worker eliminated through lean manufacturing is money back in the pockets of the bosses. The idea of making things more efficient is simply a way to enable less manpower to do the same job. In a world where you cannot cut costs on materials or raise your prices to gain profit, there is only one resource to draw from. That would be reducing labor costs by eliminating jobs.

They came in like lions at a fresh kill. They started with our plant manager and picked him apart. He was not the kind of person who was willing to do their bidding. What they were asking was to rip the family up piece by piece and see who survived. They dug into his charges and found weakness in the business practices—the orders, the continued waste, the lack of real supervision in the departments, and the continued lack of discipline. No one was ever even written up for anything. There were no paper trails to fire anyone. He did not like to use the authority he was given to enforce the rules. That was a mistake, because what it created was a "we can do what we want" attitude. That now was going to hurt the ones who did not like the policy guidelines. They forced him to one round of layoffs; it was done by seniority. The newest members of the family were rounded up, walked to the gate, and bid farewell. Within a month, he drew an early retirement, and most of his office crew went with him.

For a little while, Big Ben ran the show as they mulled their next move. We were carrying on as rumors swirled and plant closings started. The detergent plant was closed first. It had made no money in a long time, and it was thought to be too old to reform. This meant the people as well as the equipment. Profits for our parent company started falling off. The grocery chain no longer sold the cheapest product on the market and had not made up the ground with good customer service. The family all became nervous at what would happen next. This was why the lean group had been brought in. Their job was to squeeze as much profit as they could out of the old plants. This meant overhauling them all.

Then the Mexican arrived. He was a lean person himself in stature. He had a bald head and a serious nature that was unsettling to most, but not me. He spoke directly and was a confrontational person with his subordinates. He was hated instantly and with good reason: he was walking with an ax, and the family knew it. He was not like our kind-hearted plant manager; he would find your weakness and drive you out. We had some folks up and quit rather than go through what came next. Total explanation for everything you would do or say. Total accountability was expected from end to end. The supervisors squirmed as he grilled them one by one, looking for their flaws and if they knew their jobs. The Jeep exited quickly, refusing to handle the onslaught of questions of why and what. Rather than defend his actions, he unceremoniously quit. The pressure was too much for him to handle. The Tomcat feared him the most; I knew his job, and he did not.

He began to implement the lean system. It started with the 5S system. It was very good at eliminating waste, such as unneeded equipment and materials. It streamlined your tools, and by having you put things in their place, they were there when you needed them. Where before you would be searching for something, now you had it in your hands in seconds.

Motion waste was being eliminated. It provided an easier area to clean because there was no clutter. It gave the place an organized and clean appearance. The other thing that it did was free operators up to do more on the lines: either packing or quality control. This would eliminate at least one or maybe two bodies. The 5S system had a grading chart that the supervisor was responsible for. This way, they could be held to task for low scores and corrective actions given out. This would give them a reason to fire you and the paperwork to back it up.

The family bucked the system. They did not want the change. The supervisors, who had never disciplined their employees, were in trouble. If they could not get their crews to conform, they would lose their jobs first. Then someone else would come in and make them conform or get rid of them. The family was being dismantled now.

The supervisors started to be whittled down first. They were evaluated on how many people they had and if it was even required to have a supervisor for the number of people they had. One of the packer girls who had been made a supervisor was the first one to be run off. The Hawk was demoted twice, once to operator and then back to the Rat Patrol. He hung in there though, and I felt for him, as he was a good man. Nam was given another department besides tea. He was given the drink mix room to run as well as the gravy rooms. The other packer girl survived because she decided it was better to have her employees mad at her than lose her job. She wrote them up as needed. P Boy was given receiving and shipping together, and the other fellow, whom I have not mentioned up until now, was demoted. He was a Cuban fellow who was promoted during the mandate for minorities. The Tomcat himself had convinced them to let him make a little more time, and he would retire.

Now the reason the Mexican could get away with demoting and eliminating the ones who had been promoted through the mandate was he himself was a minority. He backed everything up with corrective actions and had a proper paper trail. When the first one tried to claim foul, that they were being demoted because of their race, he ripped them apart. He could use the logic that the reason headquarters had not backed him up was they preferred one minority over another. He had the paperwork to back up his motives. He was put in that place, I believe, because the California Boys realized what had happened there and knew what to do to take down the minority management. This is just my suspicion; it has never been told to me, but it did not take me long to realize that was what I was seeing.

When the Mexican and I met, I was as usual doing three things at once. He joined me on the two-pound can feeder that was situated above the can line. He introduced himself and said, "My name is Ray, but you will know me as the Mexican." Because he knew that was what he was being called. I returned the favor. I told him my name was Rick Johnson. He then asked what I was doing up there because this machine was supposed to be automatic and did not require a person to man it for fifteen minutes. I told him that the machine did not work right from the time it was bought, and no one had bothered to fix it. I then explained that if it worked right, a person could run it and move and wrap pallets, freeing up the receiving department from that task. He nodded and asked, "What was your name again? I am terrible with names."

I looked hard at him and said, "Rick, and you will never forget mine. That's because if you want something done in this department, that is the name that will always pop up!"

He then smiled at me. It shocked me. I was told that he was incapable of doing so. This guy was supposed to be so mean that not a week after he took over and moved into the corner office, a lightning storm came up. A bolt of lightning hit the guard shack not thirty yards from his office. The offices lit up with bright-white light, and the following boom was deafening and instantaneous, which is the way it is when it hits close. He was heard to say, "*Ya ha ha, you missed me again!*" They thought he had been sent from hell. I thought he was discipline driven and now accountability would be the norm, not the exception. This man would see my worth. He did just that.

He then started having production meetings where I was introduced to the five whys. This was an interrogation technique that he used to get to the root cause of a problem. It sort of went like this. Let's say you were late for work. First question: why were you late? Answer: my car wouldn't start. Second question: why would it not start? Answer: it would not turn over. Third question: why would it not turn over? Answer: the battery was dead. Fourth question: why was the battery dead? Answer: the kids got into the car and left the lights on. Fifth question: why did the kids get into car? Answer and root cause: because I did not lock the car. The problem would be corrected if they had locked the car. He used this repeatedly to find out why things were breaking down. I had learned early to give him how we were going to fix the problem after the first why. This stopped the interrogation.

To further identify problems, we started to use what was known as OEE: the overall equipment efficiency program. This helps identify root causes of downtime. It was, however, used to hold us down more than to hold us up when scores were good. In the coffee department, we had started to achieve world class scores. He tried to cheat when we achieved this goal. He tried to use our breaks and lunches against us. He should have never let me see the rule book, because I called him on it. He still insisted he was right, but he and I knew that he was cheating to not let us achieve our goal. Once you reached world class, there was no more improvements to be made unless you went to the next system. He realized the rest of the plant was not ready for that and could not implement the next step, so he tried to hold us back.

I decided to confront him. After the production meeting I went to his office. I then told him that his scores meant nothing to me if he was going to change the rules every time, we had reached our goal, and if he needed to run me off, go ahead and do so. "If you think there is someone out there who can do for you the job I am doing, feel free to go get him." I said I was tired of carrying the Tomcat anyway. I had been doing it for the last ten years, and I was sick of it. I then added, "When you do run me off, you better shred my production records and any copy of this system we are under. The California Boys might not think so, but we do have something here called the Florida Labor Board. They might be interested in the copies I have already made and the copy of the rule book you gave me, which is at my house. And see you are trying to penalize us for the breaks Florida Labor Law gives us. They may see fit after I am run off to dig into any labor violations you may have committed along the way. They may question why a person who has achieved your goals, which you set in place, is being run off. It may even warrant a lawsuit against our parent company."

I put him where I should have put the previous plant manager, in his place. He knew that he could not afford to lose me. I had finally taken enough beatings. I wasn't going to let him beat me down too. I realized my worth in this system and had the records to back it up. I had my own documentation and had been making copies all along the way for just such an occasion. The system he brought in, finally on paper, proved my worth to all who would see. The fact that I knew all the new formulas and could not be intimidated by them made me fearless and daring. I was willing to risk twenty years of service. I demanded the supervisor position. I told him maybe the California Boys would see it my way and wonder why the Tomcat was still around.

He saw it my way. Soon, the Tomcat was asked about his retirement date and if it could be moved up. After all these years, I was finally seeing the fruits of my labor come to me. The Tomcat was given a retirement party, and he retired. I was finally made supervisor. I was given a front office and then another department to run as well. My departments ran well, and I had good people working for me. I taught them the lesson I had learned. Make yourself invaluable and learn all you can. For the record, I truly cared deeply for the Tomcat. But if we were heading toward a plant closing, I wanted to have that supervisor title on my résumé.

CHAPTER 19

THE MATRIX

During this time, Cy Chung went back to China and give the quality control department to his top girl. She was a Filipina girl who was smart and very helpful to me in the transition to lean manufacturing. She had become my confidante. Gale did not care for the Mexican though. She did not trust him. She, however, went along with the changes and took part every step of the way.

Now because our parent company continued to lose sales, it was pulling the noose tighter around our necks. As their sales plunged from store to store, it became evident they were in a serious downhill slide. They had taken the customer for granted and now were paying the price. When the customers complained about long lines in the stores, they ignored them. When they complained the store's appearance was dirty, they ignored them. When customer service complaints were issued, they ignored those as well. They reasoned to a fault that the customers would complain but would keep coming back. They felt as if the customer could not get their groceries cheaper, so regardless of their complaining, they would still shop there.

What they had not counted on was the new kid on the block in the grocery business underselling us. Because they sold everything, not just groceries, they had more capital than we did. That meant they could buy in larger quantities, which meant they could buy goods cheaper. Then they could undersell us and draw the customers to the new low-price leader. The lines were long there as well, but the groceries were cheaper. When you put us head-to-head, they won. If you had to put up with poor service and long lines, at least you could spend less money doing it. Sales dropped and dropped.

Now because our sales were based solely on what the parent company moved for us; we were suffering as well. At our plant, we had never really pursued outside sales until now. It was reasoned that we had enough to keep up with supplying our parent company. This was no longer the case. We could have used the outside sales to help us stay alive. We set about pursuing what the parent company would let us pursue. It took a long time to round up outside business. It was a slow process. I prayed it was not too late.

Finally, one Friday afternoon, the Mexican approached me and told me that there would be a supervisors' meeting at eight the next morning. He said to bring a pad and paper, the list of employees under me, and their timesheets for the past year. I knew what was going to happen and was powerless to stop it.

I arrived early the next morning to find Gale making coffee. I went to her and said, "I guess I know what this is about." She said nothing and just nodded her head. I poured a cup and looked over to see Nam coming in. I poured him a cup, and the look in his eyes said it all. We knew we were there to cut heads. Big Ben came in and tried to hide his concern, but I knew him. He cared for us all as much as Mr. Johnson had. He did not, toward the middle of the meeting, hide his emotions from me. Finally, the spice room supervisor showed up with the new leader of the Rat Patrol. We were all there, plus the new buyer, who was a smart guy. He had gone and achieved his bachelor's degree. He was the production planner as well, and I worked well with him.

Then the Mexican came in with some sheets of paper. He handed them out. They had each employee's name in alphabetical order vertically. Running across the top was each job position in the plant. Squares were made to correspond for each person and position. There were blank spaces at the end, and one marked attendance. He had made his own board up front, large enough for us to see from our chairs.

He began by telling us that we all knew that our orders were down. We had people just scrubbing machines and not making us any money. He then told us that to make a budget, people would have to be let go. He stated that we would continue the process until five were gone. He started with the first name. He asked questions of each supervisor that the position in the slot indicated. If it was a position in your department, you had to say whether the employee on the list could do the job. If they could, they were awarded an x. If they could not perform the job, no mark was given. As the list went on, each supervisor would say yes or no to the questions. When you reached the attendance box, if there were no write-ups for that person for being late or absent, they were awarded an x. Tardy would be given a single line, and absent you received no mark at all. So, the process went.

During different parts of the meeting, emotions started to run a little high. This was because at times there were disputes as to whether an employee could do the job or not. This was hard for supervisors because the people who were going to be let go had been with the company a long time. How long you had been with the company had no bearing on the matrix. The Mexican only wanted the strongest players. The only time seniority played a role was if it was a tie score between employees. Each slot an employee had would later become the difference in having a job or not.

Hours wore on, and at 1:00 p.m., after we had taken just one coffee break, it was over. The matrix was complete, and the weakest players had been eliminated. Nam was upset. All five had come from his departments. This was due, in part, to the fact that he had received some ladies from company headquarters who worked in the cafeteria.

The company had decided to spend millions just about two years before to revamp and dress up headquarters. The glass palace was constructed, and the old cafeteria was eliminated. Our sales were okay at the time, so we were asked to make room for the cafeteria workers. The old plant manager had done so, obliging them. Most of these ladies had been with the company for many years. When they came to us, they were content to learn one job, and that was it. That, however, was what made them weak in the matrix.

On Monday, paperwork was sent down to headquarters, and by Tuesday, layoff packages were available. They sent a human resource person from down the street with the packages to see that things were done correctly. What we did not know in Saturday's meeting was that the Mexican was getting rid of our HR manager and our safety manager as well. We were informed of this at the production meeting Tuesday morning. Since these were manager positions, it fell on him to make these cuts. We were informed that we would absorb their jobs. We would be responsible for all safety programs, and if we had an HR problem that could not be solved, either he would solve it, or we would take it to headquarters. He then said that at 10:00 a.m. after the layoffs were complete, we would have a meeting with the plant.

Some of the employees had somehow gotten wind of Saturday's meeting. They knew something was up, but just which people were going to be let go, they had not a clue. Nam was asked to go one by one, get his employees, and bring them to the conference room. They were told that they were being let go and given their walking papers. Gale and the lady supervisor from the spice room were given the task of escorting them to their lockers. There, they would be given a box to put their things in and then escorted to the gate. No contact with anyone was allowed. They did not want them to start anything on the way out.

They were all upset that their well-paying jobs were gone. They knew their skill set would never let them see that type of money again. At our plant, if you had been with the company for fifteen years or so, you were making $16.50 an hour putting tea bags in a box. In 2001, this was good money. This, I will discuss a little later.

The HR manager who had warned me of the winds of change had been caught up in the whirlwind. He was an older man with quite a few years with the company, and it hurt him deeply to be let go. I had wondered on Saturday why he was not present at the meeting, because he was the HR person there. I had mistakenly reasoned that he was just going to be informed of the decisions and would be asked to carry them out. As it turned out, he was one of the casualties. His degree did not save him, and the company did not absorb him at headquarters. He was asked to gather his things and escorted to the gate by the new buyer.

Ten o'clock came, and the plant assembled in the break room. The mood was somber and sad. When the Mexican entered the room, he was greeted with boos. He was not fazed by it. He was used to wearing the black hat. He knew that being the bad guy came with the territory. He asked everyone to simmer down, and then he commenced to explain what had just happened. He told them what we were told, and that it was all done fairly. He did not explain the matrix or go into the detail involved with how it worked. He said he was saddened by what had just been done, but it was necessary for the plant's survival. He said that we should grieve for our lost coworkers but needed to carry on with our jobs. He then said, "From now on, to go to your supervisors with your safety issues and HR problems." He told everybody to go back to work, and we would hope that this sort of thing was not needed again. The plant did not believe him.

We then attended an operators' meeting immediately thereafter. He carried on as if nothing had happened. Some of the operators wept. These people were our friends and coworkers. I felt bad; I was part of this process now. This was not what I had hoped for when I became supervisor. This was the bad part of the job. I had hoped things like this would not come to pass, but here it was right in our laps. It was one thing to dismiss a problem employee who essentially had fired themselves. It was another to get rid of folks who had come to work and done their jobs for years. I felt responsible in some way. Could I have done something to have prevented this?

I came to the realization that I could not protect people who did not work in my departments, but I sure as hell could protect mine. I called my own meeting to take place after lunch. We all met in the coffee room. At this time, I had fifteen employees. I gathered my employees close and began to tell them how the others were eliminated. I told them that the matrix was their only means of survival. I could no longer look at the plant as if we were all one family. For the sake of my departments, I had to make them aware of how the process was being done and how to protect themselves. I had to protect their livelihoods as long as I could.

I said, "This is a sad day. I hoped it would not come to this. No matter what the Mexican just told you in that meeting, we will see this again. I have not been told this, but the matrix was not created for one-time use. It is now, I regret to tell you, our departments against the plant." I continued, "You must learn as many jobs as possible. If we get slow, don't ask to go home. I will go to the other supervisors and ask them to see if any of their employees want to go home. If it is a job, you have not done, learn it. We will go through a rotation until each of you learns the new job, then seek out another, and do it again." I added, "If you know we are going down early, go find a person whose job you don't know, tell them we are going down early, and see if they want to go home. I will talk with their supervisors."

One of my guys said, "What good will it do? They are going to shut us down in the end anyway."

I responded, "It will keep you off unemployment until then and help you feed your family. If there is a job in either of our departments that you don't know, let's start with learning them."

I would build the strongest team in the plant. This was all I could do: forewarn them. The rest was up to them. I had done the math. The Mexican had just saved the plant over $300,000 for the year by the cuts he just made. I also knew that whether the orders picked up or not, he would find a way to do it again. He would do this for his own survival; he was competing against other plant managers. His eyes were on getting one of his bosses' jobs. The more profit he could show, the closer he would be to that goal, or so he thought.

In the meantime, I worked on my own matrix. You see, I also realized he had a matrix for us supervisors as well. We, of course, did not see it. I figured that we had one as well. We were also expendable. I had an edge. I could run the coffee department, and the others could not. Remember, I had worked in every department in the plant at one time or another. I set about learning the other supervisors' inventories. I, in this way, could learn what it took to run their departments. I also did everything asked of me and did not buck the Mexican. The other supervisors shirked duties when possible and Nam more than most. I went along with the program even though many a time I would have liked to have protested about some of his systems that I saw no practical value in. Life went on, and my team and I grew stronger and stronger, preparing ourselves for the inevitable.

CHAPTER 20

BIG BEN'S BREAKING POINT

It came to pass that one of the employees who had been laid off during the first seniority layoffs passed away. She was only fifty or so years old. Her name was Kate. Now Kate worked with the Rat Patrol, in the gravy rooms, and anywhere she was needed. She may have made it further had she survived the first round of layoffs. She was as kind a person as you had ever seen. Kate would bring in donuts, pastries, and sandwiches for her coworkers. It was not uncommon for her to bring in cookies and things especially around Christmas. It used to anger me that some of the guys she worked with would gladly eat her offerings and then make fun of her behind her back. She had a rather plain appearance, and her uniform did nothing to help that fact. One Christmas when we were all out on the town, Kate had worn a beautiful dress, and she looked stunning. She lived alone and on more than one occasion had missed time for her cats. When she was laid off, I felt for her, but her parents were quite wealthy, and I knew she would be taken care of.

Then one day, news came that she had passed. Her heart, which was so kind, gave away with her. As soon as the plant found out, we all started to decide to go to the funeral. She was part of the family and deserved our respect at her funeral. Upon hearing this, the Mexican decided that he would dock anyone who went and take half of a point away from you on the point system we were now under. You see, this system was applied in this way. If you were late or left early, you were given one half of a point. If you were out excused or not, you were given one whole point. Six total points meant a verbal warning. Eight and you were written up. Nine, you were given two days off, and you were to decide. Ten and you were fired, if this all occurred for one year. We were given six sick days a year, and now you would be penalized for using them. I now fell under different rules because it did not apply to management. It was wrong what the Mexican was doing. He said that the plant could not afford to lose production every time an old employee passed away.

The plant was furious, and Big Ben, who had been there thirty years by then, was pissed. I think the only reason Big Ben had stuck it out so far was he thought just maybe if he went along with the program that he would one day be plant manager. He deserved it more than any person there. This, though, was one slap in the face of tradition that he would not take lying down. He went to the Mexican's superiors. He argued that this woman was our friend and deserved our due respect.

He asked them if they did not have any morals and respect for the dead. The answer was the same one the Mexican had given. They had reasoned that for too long people had taken advantage of missing time and being late with no consequence. This now was the result of that fact. They stood with the Mexican.

At this point, Big Ben gave up on the whole situation. Many of the employees could not afford to take off for the funeral, mainly because many were at the age that doctor appointments had to be taken. They could not afford to lose their jobs; they needed all their points for the doctor visits. The plant would have strung him up and tarred and feathered him if not for one thing: the Mexican went to the funeral. He did not really know Kate; he bought flowers and took them on the plant's behalf. You see, beneath his evil demeanor was somewhere a good Catholic. He justified what he had done in this way. From then on, if a family member who either worked there or was part of some-one's family passed away, he would go. He would attend any function that required a show of respect. In his mind, he was following orders, whether it was morally right or not. He knew deep down, though, that there should be exceptions to every rule. Big Ben would not let this go and announced he would be retiring.

Although he had gone along with everything the Mexican did, he had drawn a line. Big Ben had plenty of money, and it would not be a problem for him to retire. However, he had been at the plant almost longer than anyone. That plant was a part of him, and a lot of him went into it. I felt much the same way. I was watching the rest of the family either retire and leave or just quit. The Mexican was driving them out in droves. I was determined to stay. I knew that the harassment would become worse as time went on. I wanted to be the last man standing. I was hoping that after it was all said and done, we would recover. I thought we would go on and be stronger, maybe even grow again.

We all gathered for Big Ben's retirement party, and one of the California Boys came down and gave a speech. The Mexican spoke kind words and gave Big Ben his due. I wondered as I listened if I would ever have this happen for me. Finally Big Ben got his turn to speak. His voice cracked as he wished us well. Big Ben hated to go and leave this part of his life behind. We applauded and gave him the traditional hugs that he so richly deserved. The Mexican had accomplished yet another culvert goal. He now had rid himself of the superintendent. He had saved the plant $65,000 for the year. The job was now split between the mechanics' supervisor and the rest of the supervisors who were left.

The idea was to create enough pressure and piss off the old guard to the extent they would leave. The California Boys had brought him in to do just that. Everyone that he could get to quit would save severance packages that were awarded to laid-off employees. That in turn saved the parent company money, which made him look better. He still eyed his bosses' jobs.

CHAPTER 21

THE FIGHT TO STAY ALIVE

More time elapsed, and things continued to get tougher. The Mexican kept turning up the pressure. Every time our parent company made an announcement, we held our breath. It was the same every time, more layoffs for the stores and warehouses. The company was now in full retreat to the Deep South. They began to close stores that were further north. A new CEO was brought in to right the ship. They were trying to stay alive by getting back to our core markets. They had reasoned that they had spread themselves out too far and too thin. When one of these news releases came out, it was certain that one, maybe two, manufacturing plants would be closed. We were always sure to get what was now the party line speech from the Mexican. He had stated to stay alive we must keep producing more profit. This meant what I knew it would: more heads must be cut.

Our sales had continued to fall. With each store closing, he had figured out what percentage of profit would be lost and how much production we would lose from its closing. He then would adjust the roster accordingly. He came to me and said we would be meeting Saturday morning. He told me to be thinking of someone to eliminate. I had made up my mind that none of my people were going to lose their jobs. They had done what I had asked, and they were strong in the matrix. The only thing that might hurt them was a tie where attendance was involved. I had one of my blenders who was weak in this area, and I had written him up.

When we arrived that Saturday morning, the Mexican had cooked us breakfast. In the quality control lab, we had a stove for cooking to sample our products. He had cooked us eggs, bacon, and toast. I think he knew how stressful this meeting was going to be. I guess he thought it would go better on a full stomach. After breakfast, the meeting started. The matrix was brought out and examined. My packers were all strong and could work in every area of the plant. My operators were strong as well and could run many machines in the plant. My blenders were not as strong, and my roaster was weakest of all.

The Mexican said, "Okay, I need five bodies. That is what we are looking at getting rid of today. I know this is tough, but the plant's survival is on the line." He then said for us to look at the matrix, and he identified the weakest links. He wrote these employees down on a separate board. My roaster and blender were on the list, along with eight others. He then went to each supervisor that the employees did not belong to. He would point to a name and ask the supervisor why we should or shouldn't get rid of this person. The supervisor then would make a case to get rid of that person, hopefully saving one of theirs. When all the supervisors had spoken, if the employee belonged to you, it was time to defend them. When it was over, a vote was taken to see who would be voted out; the majority ruled.

My roaster was attacked first. The spice room supervisor attacked him for his attitude and his unwillingness to work in other departments. She further stated that he was being protected under the old school rules, he was weak in the matrix, and no allowances should be made. Nam did not say much when it was his turn, just that the employee did know the roasting job, but he also did agree that he had an adjustment problem. Gale stated that she had found him to have a bad attitude, and maybe he was being looked after because he was Tomcat's and Big Ben's brother-in-law. The buyer deferred comment, stating he did not know enough about the situation. Then he added, "It is a problem, though, when we plan production, and you are not roasting; we are at a loss as to what to do with him."

The mechanics' supervisor agreed.

The Mexican looked at me and said, "Okay, Rick, why should we keep him? I have to say that I am in agreement with the things I have heard thus far."

I thought carefully; he was a thorn in my side for sure. I had to get a ration of crap from my other employees about him and his attitude every time I turned around. I then thought that I needed him. I began by saying, "How many of you in this room can roast coffee? I will tell you how many, none of you. I am the only one in this room who can roast coffee. If you look carefully at the matrix, there is only one other person in this plant who can roast coffee, and that is Dewayne.

Dewayne is our lead mechanic, and I have two departments to run. So, if we eliminate him, who will roast coffee? We have, up until now, not made the arrangements to train anybody to do so. We would need six months to train a new roaster. Do we have the time and resources to do so? I think this is an exception to the matrix, and until we can free someone up to learn to roast, he needs to stay."

The Mexican looked around the room and asked for a show of hands. "Who says go?" The spice room supervisor raised her hand. She knew that I had made my case, but at least she could say she voted for him to be let go after the fact. This would shed some good light on her for her employees. She had three up on the board, and Gale had one as well. I thought Gale would vote for him to be let go, but she did not. She was smart enough to know my argument was correct. Everybody else followed suit, and he was allowed to stay.

My blender was then attacked. He was tied with another person and had no x in his attendance box. I had written him up for being out too much. He had done what he needed in the matrix but had fallen in the point system trap. Now how could I save him? I had told him that there might be a provision in the Family Medical Leave Act for him. I had told him to apply for this as soon as I found out about the meeting. The last absence was because his son was sick, and he had been to the doctor and had documentation to back it up. Remember, we handled our HR problems. If they ruled in his favor, I could retract the point and the write-up. So, when everybody was asked, they agreed that according to the matrix rules, he was the weakest link. The Mexican did not like this blender of mine to boot. I then countered that you could not eliminate him because he had a pending case with the HR department. I stated that if he won the case and had the write up retracted and we had canned him because of his position in the matrix, we were looking at a lawsuit. I assured them I knew him, and he would pursue legal action. The person he was tied with was eliminated.

When it was said and done, I lost nobody. The spice room supervisor lost two, Gale lost one, and Nam lost one. It was decided that one from the Rat Patrol would be eliminated as well. I had not cheated to keep my people; I just had taken precautions to keep my group strong. On my way down from the conference room, the mechanics' supervisor said I should have been a lawyer. He looked at Gale and said, "We didn't count on our employees having a lawyer. I think next time I am bringing my attorney with me."

Gale laughed and said, "Me too."

I just laughed and said, "I still have my folks."

After the meeting, everybody went home. The Mexican asked me to hang around a bit. He asked me to go get some lunch with him. I had been to lunch with him and the other supervisors before but not him alone. I agreed, and we went to a local eatery.

When we arrived, he ordered a beer and asked me if I wanted one. I said, "No. Give me a Turkey and Coke."

He took a sip of his beer and said, "You were pretty slick in that meeting. I did not know your blender was going down to HR at headquarters."

I replied, "It just came up late Friday afternoon; I did not have a chance to tell you."

He then asked, "I guess that it was just happenstance that he went right before this meeting? Did you sign off on the paperwork for him to go ahead with it?"

I then said, "Yes, and he took the paperwork after work straight down to headquarters to their HR department. I told him he might as well, no sense putting it off." I took a good swallow of my drink. "You okay with that, boss? I mean, it was the right thing to do." I continued, "His kid was at the doctor; he has a legitimate case. He also brought me documentation to back it up."

He smiled that evil grin. "I tell you what; if you will go to some classes I have lined up for you, the company will pay for it."

I said, "Sure what are they for?"

He said, "They are college classes in leadership. I think they will serve you well. I really think you should go after a degree. I don't know what they will approve down the street, but we will get you what we can."

I said, "Let me take the one, and we can go from there."

He said, "Great. Go Monday and sign up for them and bring me the paperwork."

I agreed, and we sat and had a few. He hit me with some plan B scenarios if the plant was to close.

He wanted me to go into business with him. He wanted to start a coffee business if our plant failed. I listened carefully. I was wary of him. He wanted to buy our old roasters and sell to the prisons and such. He had some interesting ideas, I had to admit. Where was the capital coming from though? I had a good idea he wanted a full partner and my money. I just let him talk. Finally, when it was time to go, he said, "One other thing, you will be running the tea department as well as your other departments from now on."

I asked, "What about Nam?"

He said, "I want him to concentrate on the gravy rooms. They are lagging way behind; I am writing him up Monday and giving him two months to turn them around."

I knew what that meant. I would be running tea from then on; he would not bring Nam back in to do it.

Monday, after I got my departments together and went to the 8:00 a.m. supervisors' meeting, I left to go sign up for my course. While I was gone, Nam was written up and told what was going to happen. Nam had been there a long time and never had been written up. The problem was his gravy room crew. They had run over the last two supervisors and were running over him as well. They bucked every program and fought the Mexican every step of the way. They did not realize it, but the gravy train was coming to a halt. Their actions were going to get Nam fired.

When I came back, I went to Nam's office by the tea department to find him cleaning off his desk. I went in and told him I was sorry about what was happening. As he took down his Georgia football memorabilia, he told me not to worry about it. He said he knew I was doing like I was told, and it was not my fault. He then said other than the mechanic, I knew tea as well as anybody. He said, "Hell, you started off there for four years. Now it is yours to run. You know where everything is you need; you have been covering for me when I went off on vacations for over two years now. I am going to set up shop in the gravy office where I can be close to them and not close to that damn Mexican."

With that, he took the picture of his wife and kid off the desk and left. I felt bad for him. He was still old school, and he did not like to write people up. If he wanted a job, however, he was going to have to hand out some write-ups. I knew he wouldn't.

I left his office and went to the spice room supervisor's office. She was busy doing some paperwork. I knocked on the glass window and stuck my head in the door. I asked her if she had a minute. She said she would be through soon, so we could get together then.

I said, "Sure. Come to my office when you are done here."

I went to my office, and she arrived shortly thereafter. She entered, and I asked her to have a seat. I started by saying, "I guess you know about Nam." She said she did. I then asked her if she knew where this thing was heading. She told me she had a good idea it was the end of the road for Nam. I told her that was my suspicion as well.

I then said, "I don't think he can cut us any further in the supervisor area. So it will be you and me running the whole plant." I continued, "I think we should prepare ourselves for what is coming."

She then asked, "How do you propose we do that?"

I said, "The gravy train people are the problem. They have managed to run off three supervisors, if they run Nam off too. One of us will get that department if Nam fails." Then I told her my plan. I suggested that we cross-train our departments further, making them stronger. My idea was to combine the coffee, tea, and spice departments to make them stronger than the gravy room folks in the matrix.

More layoffs were surely coming. In that way, the problem children might be eliminated without having to go through a bunch of write-ups and red tape. I further explained that we had people in our departments who could work gravy, but gravy did not have people who could work ours. They protested so much when they were asked to work in the other departments that rather than force the issue, the other supervisors had left them alone. I was trying now to secure our jobs. She agreed with me, and we shook on it and made plans for how we would go about it.

Tuesday came, and with it, the layoffs that had been arranged Saturday. Nam had arranged to take the day off. I was given the unpleasant task of rounding up his employees and the one from shipping. I walked them up front with my arm around them, trying to console them as best I could. I escorted them one by one to the conference room and was asked to sit in as they were being let go. I then escorted them to their lockers, watched as they emptied them, and then walked them to the gate. It was tough to do. I had worked with these folks for many years.

The shipping employee, Lurch had just bought a house; he was very upset. I had advised my employees not to make any major purchases for the past year just in case. Gale's employee was a guy, so I wound up going to his locker with him. It was Bert, the last of the Who Ha Clan. When we got to the gate, he had tears in his eyes, as did I. I hugged his neck and wished him well.

At 10:00 a.m., we gathered again in the conference room. The Mexican was again greeted with boos. He, as he had done before, explained the need for the layoffs. He told of store and warehouse closings and how we were lucky that we had done the things we had to do to stay in a job. He was sorry, but that was the way it was. He was then asked if there were going to be more layoffs. He flatly told them that it depended on what the parent company did. He told them that it might be that more layoffs were needed to survive if they closed more stores. He said, "You know by now how to make yourself a strong player. There is not a lot separating the plant in the matrix now. You are the strongest team yet. That is why you are still here." He then told us that Nam would be focusing on gravy and that I would run the tea department. If anyone had any problems or needed information and worked in tea, from then on, they were to report to me. With that, he dismissed us and told us to go and put our minds on our work.

We then went to the production meetings. My other two departments were first and had no issues. The tea department operators were next, and things were running well there. I then asked them into my office. I told them that it was not my intent to take over tea. I had known and respected Nam for over twenty-three years. I further told them that the last thing I really wanted was ten more employees with ten more sets of issues. I was getting no more money for the extra headache.

I then proceeded to tell them what I wanted from them and how I was going to cross-train every employee in my departments. I told them that when they were down, they would go to the spice room as well and learn any job in there. That was met with opposition from one of my operators. He wanted to know why he had to go to the spice department. It was not one of my departments. I told him I had reached an agreement with the spice room supervisor, and I was trying very hard to keep from walking employees to that gate. "Take my advice and do as I ask. It may save your job, at least until all this blows over or until they shut us down." I then went to the tea department, gathered the packers and blender, and told them as well.

CHAPTER 22

SCHOOL IS IN

The next two months found me going to leadership classes for supervisors. When that was through, I was sent for Microsoft Office classes, and then I started Excel classes. Then I went back for Microsoft advanced classes and intermediate Excel. For that time, these were new programs. In the meantime, I was taught more formulas and business solution techniques by the Mexican. I learned about all kinds of spaghetti charts, flowcharts, and fishbone solution diagrams. I was learning a great deal of things now, and I have to say I was refreshed by it.

It was new for me, to finally have someone really encouraging me to learn different things and paying me to do so. It was then suggested for me to start doing payroll. I dabbled in it but really could not find time to do it. He wanted me to be familiar with that program. We had a lady to do it, and she was quite good at it. I was willing to learn as much as I could in any area of the plant. I became immersed in finance. I knew what was coming in and how much was going out.

I knew the profit margins and what it was taking to keep them. I was glad to get up every day and learn something new.

For all those years, I had been held back. Now I was like a kid in a candy store. I had access to all records and paperwork. I was inside and part of the top chain of command. Had it not been for the Mexican coming in and things being shaken up, I would have been lucky to have just made supervisor. I was out of my cage now and looking for anyway to help the plant make more money. I wanted to revive us in some way and make us strong. I felt if I could get us to hang on a little while longer, the parent company would recover. If they recovered and we were still giving them profits, we would be saved. I believed this and was not letting myself think otherwise.

In the meantime, I was dealing with my departmental issues. The roaster was giving me problems. I had told him at the last round of layoffs that his job was put into question. I told him his attitude need-ed to change, and it was not going to be possible to just keep him in coffee. He needed to learn other jobs. He had been around as long as I had, maybe a few years more. It was true he was related to Tomcat and Big Ben. That fact had preserved him so far before I took over. Not long after he was roaster, he almost blew the plant up. That resulted in me calling the fire department because of the explosion. It had de-stroyed one roaster and caught the roasting area on fire. This was not the type of fire you were going to pick up a hose and put out. I had to evacuate the plant. Then, I had to explain what had happened and to attend a hearing from the parent company—with OSHA in atten-dance. Their safety manager wanted to know exactly what happened.

At that time, I was not the supervisor, but because I knew more about what had happened, it fell on me to do the talking.

You would have thought they would have taken him off the roasters, which would have been the best thing to do. It had been his fault. He had overloaded the roaster and became confused as to what to do. Then he compounded the problem by resetting the cylinder that was packed with flaming coffee, resulting in the explosion. Instead, the Tomcat and the old plant manager decided to let him stay on them. Nevertheless, he became my problem when I took over.

When I told him what he needed to do, I was met with back talk. He was trying to give me reasons he should stay in the roasting area and do things there. I told him I had run the roasters for fifteen years, and I knew when it was time to do things to them. I also told him the timeline was not the same, as we were not putting as many roasting hours on them now. I further told him I was keeping records as to roasting hours, and I would decide when it was time to do needed maintenance on them. He still argued with me. I finally became frustrated trying to reason with him and told him, "You will start going to other departments to get in rotation with the other employees." Then I said it was the end of the discussion.

I went to the Mexican right after that and told him I would like to free up my best operator to learn to roast. One way or another, I was going to eliminate this problem. I figured he would either get in line when I started training somebody else at roaster or quit. I was only asking him to do what the rest of the employees were already doing. I knew he had been there a long time, but that was not reason enough for him to do nothing when the others rotated. I did not have work for him in the department, and we needed people elsewhere to keep the plant running. He had been babied along by the Tomcat and Big Ben, and now to be fair, I had to resolve the issue. My other employees never missed a chance to remind me of his bad attitude and him continuing to buck rotation.

I managed to free up Red. He was my best operator and a good mechanic as well. He had learned to operate anything you put him on and learn it quick. I, at first, let the roaster train him for a little while. Then I stepped in, and with me and Dewayne, we were able to train him rather quickly. In the meantime, the older roaster was put into the rotation. He protested and was mad every time, but I was doing what I had to do. I could not tolerate having one of my employees not playing with the rest of the team. I would not let him back me into a corner because I had no other roaster to go to anymore.

On one occasion, he was sent to the spice room to stack off. It was not a hard job, and I had asked the spice room supervisor to see to it that whatever he was put on he could handle. She had done as I had asked and put him on the easiest thing she had. The problem was that day, one of my other employees went somewhere he would have rather gone. We were not roasting, and the other employee left first to where they needed him. I was then called for my roaster to fill another position that had just come up. I told him where to go, and he just frowned at me.

In about two hours, he came to me and said he had enough of this place and was going home. He said he was fed up and was done. I asked him what he meant. He said he was sick of the spice room and the plant, so he was going home. I tried to convince him to stay. I told him to go back to the spice room and stick it out. He just refused and left. Soon the spice room supervisor came to me and wanted to know where he was. What could I say? He left?

When the Mexican found this out, he said he had to be at the very least written up. I guess he thought better of his actions and returned to work the next day. As soon as the supervisor's meeting was over, he was written up. He was very upset and said he felt as if he was being stepped on. I reasoned with him. "How is it you feel this way? Every person in this plant has to work into the rotation. I and the spice room supervisor both must work on the lines at times to get things done. You should not have left your workstation. You need to realize we all must pull together to make this work." I wasn't including the gravy train. They were their own problem to be dealt with in time. He accepted the write-up.

In just a few weeks, he came to me with the key to the roaster tool cabinet. He said, "I just quit. I don't need this place anymore. Here's your key, and I don't have any use for you anymore either." He continued, "When I was written up, you could have prevented it."

I told him, "Rev, I saved you from being laid off six months ago. You did this, not me. How was I supposed to save you?"

He said, "You could have said I was sick."

I looked straight at him and said, "You were not sick."

He said, "No, but you could have said I was."

I then said, "Then you wanted me to lie?"

He said nothing. He just turned and left. What I have not mentioned until now was the fact that he was a preacher of a small church.

The wanting me to lie comment, I guessed, would stick with him a while. I had handled it the best way I could, and it was not easy to see someone of those years leave. I reasoned though I had tried to change him, and he would not change. I had told him of the consequences of not conforming, and he chose not to.

In this time frame, Nam's sixty days were up. He had made some improvement but not enough. His crew continued to fight him. The Mexican brought him in and gave him another month. He had already put in for vacation way in advance to any of these current problems he had and was granted his vacation. The thirty days would start after that. The spice room supervisor and I were asked to take turns filling in. I guess the Mexican was feeling us out to see who Nam's replacement would be. I already had three departments; she only had spice and the mill rooms. I thought maybe it would be her. I don't know how he thought he would do it, but we were both asked to cover. Perhaps more cross-training for us both. We decided on the last day to go over there together. We both attended the production meeting.

I was shocked at the way they behaved. They openly barked at the Mexican and were ill prepared at the meeting. They did not have their facts straight, and after some careful questioning on the Mexican's behalf, I could tell they were not telling the truth. They were trying to blame the blender for something he had not done. Their numbers did not add up with the time they had logged. They were manipulating their time sheets. The Mexican knew this; of course, he just looked at me as if to say, "Sic 'em."

He said, "That's all I have today. Have a good weekend." He asked if the spice room supervisor or I had something to add. I then asked the Mexican if he minded leaving. He nodded and left.

There were three operators there. I said to them, "Who is it you think you are fooling?"

They just looked at each other. I grabbed a time sheet and asked one, "Do you know what I am holding?"

One said, "It is a timesheet."

I said, "Yes and it's something else too. It is a company document." I then stated the fact that falsifying a company document was grounds for immediate dismissal. They looked as if they were going to be sick. I said, "Let me tell you all something: the Mexican knows what you are doing, and your time is running out."

The spice room supervisor added that he was not one to be fooled.

I then said, "I was here when you said the blender let you run out of product. He did not let one line run out of product. He was not there to defend himself, and rather than call you all out as liars, I let it slide." I added, "It was the first and last time that either myself or the spice room supervisor will let something slide. You guys are on the verge of getting Nam run off. He is a good man, and it pisses me off! I promise you that will not happen to me or her. I will not lose my job because of you or anybody in this department. If you think I am play- ing with you, be assured I am not. If he is run off, it is you to blame for taking advantage of his good nature." I then closed with "The gravy train is over. Either get in line or find yourself another line of work. You either conform under Nam, or you will conform under whoever is next. That goes for every person in this department. Get back to your lines and never write something down that is untrue again."

When we walked off, the spice room supervisor asked me if I thought they got the message. I said, "I don't know, but they may as well face facts. I don't think Nam will do what is required to get them turned around. It is going to take firing one to get their attention."

The reason they acted the way they did is because nobody had fired any of them yet. They had not even been written up for anything. After a week with them, I had seen a lot of things that our departments had for a year, or more been shed of. Nam had covered for them and was going down in flames because of it. I then told her, "I am not letting them have an inch."

She responded in kind. It was, as I told her, us or them.

The month went by, and Nam could not bring his numbers up and could not get the gravy train to conform. Someone from HR headquarters came down, and Nam was let go. He shook my hand and said, "I just could not do what he wanted. I think he only wants two supervisors anyway, and it would not have mattered what I had done."

I told him I was sorry to see him leave and would miss him. I now had seniority on the whole plant; only Nam had been there longer. The Mexican decided to give the spice room supervisor the gravy department. I thought it was because I had three, and she only had one. I was wrong. He had other plans. I told her I would back her up in anything she did.

At the same time, another CEO was brought in to the parent company to take over, and with that came new store and plant closings. You know by now what that meant for us. The plant knew this time before we had even arranged the meeting. One of my packing ladies came to me and did something no one had done before. She asked that if there was to be another layoff she be let go. She said she could no longer bare the strain and wanted her time to be now. I understood and asked her if she was sure. I told her she was one of my best workers, and she would be missed greatly. She told me she had already made some arrangements to work at a day care that her daughter was at. I then asked her one more time if she was sure this is what she wanted. With tears in her eyes, she said yes. I hugged her neck and said I would ask the Mexican.

At the next supervisors' meeting, I informed the Mexican. I then asked him if my girl could be let go as one of the next layoffs because we all knew it was what was coming. He asked, "Why?"

I told him she had had enough. I then said, "I think this is something at this point that could be asked of any packer. Then the ones that stay want to stay. It would let someone keep a job maybe that they would have lost."

They agreed with me, and she was slated to be laid off. It came. The other three came from the gravy train. We had picked out the worst, and because of their position in the matrix, it was an easy pick. This was done in less than two hours this time. My plan had worked to get rid of some of the problem children. Maybe this would make the new gravy supervisor's job easier.

Now this time, when it came to walk them to the gate, I did not feel so bad for the ones let go. They had been fairly warned and had pushed it to the very limit. I had seen three supervisors put on the road for their actions. The only thing that we did not expect was that the mechanic thought he should get the department not the spice room supervisor. He was one of the ring leaders in the defiance group. He then, in protest at not getting the job, decided to not come to work until he was fired under the point system. He thought he would go to HR down the street and get a transfer after he was already fired. He went with the feeling the point system was unfair, and they would see it his way and just transfer him. The parent company was letting people go daily; they did not see it his way, and he was then gone.

CHAPTER 23

A LITTLE HOPE

Some time passed, and the new CEO waited to see what results his previous changes would bring. In this time, we went about running the plant. I held out hope that we had made it through four other manufacturing plants closing along with numerous warehouses and distribution centers. We were still alive. The Mexican had leaned out the plant to the point we were still turning out a good profit with the sales we had. Our sales at one time in our heyday netted eleven million dollars' worth of profit to our parent company. We were now lucky to do four.

We had tried every avenue of generating outside sales. I thought if we could, on our own, generate more profit for the parent company, they would see our worth and keep us. Then a congresswoman from Georgia contacted us. She wanted us to produce a drink mix packet for the troops and for the prison system. She also wanted us to produce bulk coffee for the military bases. I thought this might be what I was waiting for. This was a way to stay alive.

When she came, I was the one who escorted her around, to show her our plant and explain to her how we could do what she wanted. I went into detail as to how we could do this for her. I knew everything she wanted to do was feasible. I joked and laughed with her, as when she spoke, she was down home. By that, I mean when she opened her mouth cornbread and grits would come out. She was as southern as you would expect for a Georgia girl who came from a small town. I offered her coffee or iced tea at the end of our tour. I then asked her when she would need to be leaving. She said she was going to Washington the following day. I asked where she was staying. It was a local hotel close to the plant. I then boldly asked if she would be so kind as to join my wife and me for dinner that evening. I told her I knew a place to get some fried catfish or shrimp. She agreed, and I gave her my home phone number.

I cringed as I let her talk to the Mexican. He was brash, and at times, he did not even understand the southern slang she used. Nevertheless, he was okay with her, and as she departed, she said she would see me tonight. The Mexican just smiled, and after she left, he asked what she was talking about. I said, "No offense but it's time for some charm, and you, sir, don't have any!"

He replied, "You ain't going to sleep with her, are you?"

I joked as she was an older lady, "I might have to take one for the team." I then told him I had asked her to supper with my wife and me.

That evening found us in a small restaurant that served fresh seafood. She was glad to get it. She said many times on the road you did not get fresh seafood or southern cooking. The food was great. I kept my conversation to things other than the plant for a good bit of the night. Her dad had been a farmer; my dad had grown up farming. We, as kids, had to work a couple of acres my uncle had, and she could relate. We drank cocktails, and she listened to my wife tell how things were where she had lived. She was a northern girl who had grown up in Indiana. She seemed as fascinated with her stories as my wife was with her thick southern accent.

As the night wore on, I felt it was time to ask her some questions about how she had come to seek us out. She had explained that the government was always looking for cheaper ways to mass produce things. She had been sent with the task to seek out a cheaper supplier than the one they were now using. I then queried as to how much volume we were talking about. The numbers were huge. I asked her how we could move this forward. I told her that I did not mean to beg, but we were in danger of the plant closing, and this would be just what we needed to save it.

She responded with "Let me get you some poundage and unit sizes. Then you can work me up a quote to show my boss."

I assured her I would find a way for us to get it to them cheaper and on time. With that, we drove her to the hotel. My wife and I assured her meeting her was a pleasure. We bid her farewell, and I said I hoped to see her again soon.

Two days later, the information came in, and the Mexican had me do a labor study and cost sheet. I cut it as close as I could; I had to undersell the competition. I crunched numbers all day. I worked up a proposal and had every base covered. We crossed our fingers and submitted it. She called us back and said it looked good. She had her boss look at it, and he thought it was good as well. Now it had to go back to our parent company for them to approve us doing it. The profit margin was about 27 percent, and it would breathe life into our company. We could lock in to being busy all the time; new equipment could be bought. So it went to headquarters, and we waited. We waited and waited some more. A month had passed and no word yet. I wanted to know what the holdup was.

The Mexican pushed the issue but to no avail. We were not being given an answer as to what the deal was. The person who was over our plant down the street was stonewalling us. They kept saying that it was on this one or that one's desk. They had their reasons. I could not understand why with the money that was laid out in front of them, they were not pursuing this. The Mexican had said that perhaps it was because it was a government contract. I wanted answers, and I wasn't getting any. I had asked if I could call down the street and start pursuing this myself. I was told no, that to pressure them anymore was a bad move for the plant.

More time elapsed. I was now beginning to think that there was something underlying that was causing this not to go through. Had the Mexican made them mad or something? I talked to the congresswoman to see if she could do something. She was given the same runaround and even told me that she did not have long before she would have to pursue another supplier. I told her I understood it was business but to please hold on a little longer. She said she could hold them off for a while, but she did not know how long. I did not want her in trouble. She had done her part. It was the parent company that did not do theirs. Why was all I could ask myself. The answer was there, but I did not want to believe it. It could only be that they were eyeing us for shutdown.

I knew we were still giving them profit though, and that was the part that did not fit into the puzzle. I had figured if it ever came a time that we were underbid or failed to produce a profit, it was over. I also knew our business, and I knew we could not be underbid. It was impossible to run any leaner and get supplies any cheaper. I deduced there was one more step the Mexican could take, and that was it. We could go just a little smaller; it meant the complete destruction of what was our company.

Temps could be brought in to do the packing jobs, and our packers could be eliminated. We would need full-time operators, mechanics, and blenders, but the packing positions could be farmed out. The thought of doing this displeased me. When I had written up the proposal, I had figured to use some temps to get the job done along with one roaster, one blender, and one operator. That was that, but to get rid of all general labor was a different story. I had hoped that my crew could stay strong, and my packers would be saved by us coming out of the parent company's hole. I had promised them that if they learned more positions in the matrix, their jobs would be secure if the plant was open.

When the idea of temps was mentioned to me early in the Mexican's tenure, my response was that it was not fair. He had stated that the hourly wage that the packers were making was too high. I said it was, but the wage they were making was a result of hard work, dedication, and loyalty to our company. When these people started out, they started with a modest salary. It was good enough to have some things like a home and a car. Over the years, they stayed with the company and were given raises, and as time passed, it had accumulated into good money for what they were doing. I then told him that what I could see coming out of using staffing agencies was the erosion of the workforce. He asked, "How?"

I said, "Well, let's start by you are barely making a living with a staffing agency. You, in many cases, would have no benefits, no insurance for you or your family and no security. No profit sharing, no 401(k), nothing but an hourly wage job that does not even guarantee you will work in the same place as you did the day before."

He had argued that might be true, but from a running the company standpoint, you could make more profit with cheaper labor.

I said, "So what you are saying is that unless you are in a skilled position or have a degree, you don't deserve to be making a good living?"

He said, "Then you should get yourself to a better place through education."

I asked, "What is wrong with getting yourself to the better place by giving time and effort and sweat and dedicating yourself to your company?" I then reminded him that he could go to school from now to doomsday, but he would never begin to learn what I and some of the others had learned from on-the-job training. "You are from the 'it looks good on paper, so it must work' type crowd, and I am from the 'you know it works because you have done it' crowd."

He agreed that was true, but he was running a company for the bosses down the road, and they wanted to see profits on a paper. He continued, "They don't see people; they see dollars and cents."

I agreed that we disagreed on this issue.

This was what my father had forewarned me about, and I was seeing it staring me right in my face. He was, as usual, right in his assumptions as to where companies were heading and that we were now numbers without faces on a piece of paper. I thought this was not to be true, but it was. I knew as I fumed over not getting this government contract that somewhere down the street, somebody was crunching numbers to get rid of us. Someone was plotting to do us in, and I was powerless to do anything about it. If I just had a forum, some way to talk to them, some way I could be heard. I was wondering if a letter to the CEO might be heard. Then I reasoned that if I overstepped my boundary, I could be fired. I was left in a wait-and-see situation.

Then news came that the California Boys were leaving. The remaining plant managers were assembled, and they said they were told the Boys were going back to the west coast. I took it as either they had finished what they started and were moving on, or they had failed. They were being let go by the parent company. I thought this was a bad sign as well. I reasoned that the parent company was going to go ahead and close the remaining plants and be done with us all. My brain told me this was what was happening, but my heart did not want to believe it.

The Mexican said he thought that they had put in the lean plans and were done, so the parent company no longer needed them. I don't know whether he knew better or not. He was going to tell me anything to keep me from leaving.

The next day, his boss came by to say goodbye. I met him at the front door by chance. I shook his hand and looked him straight and hard in the eye. I said, "I wish you luck, sir."

He responded, "Thank you, Rick. You have done some great things here and made great strides." He knew who I was and had never met me. His eyes told me all that I needed to know. They were going to do us in. I wish that was one trait that I did not have, that I could look into his eyes and see his heart. His eyes and the nervousness in his voice told me that he knew what was going to happen.

He knew that we had busted our butts to do their bidding, and we still were going to lose. They had told us from the beginning that if we did as they asked, we would keep our jobs. Now I could see in this man's eyes, he was embarrassed by what he had said and done. He had failed and had failed us. I felt sick and ashamed after all the sacrifice and the people who had lost their jobs, and for what? To be shut down anyway.

I walked to the roasting area where there was no one. I needed to sort out my feelings. I hoped my intuition was wrong. I weighed one thing against the other. The Mexican had already done the math as to what would happen next and what we would do to survive. It would be as I mentioned before, no packers and we could still give them about three million in profit. Would we be given that chance?

They had come out and measured the roof and the plant. I knew it was either to get us a new roof or use the cost of getting a new one for a reason to shut us down. Then I figured what a lot of people did not know that we were on the same lease as headquarters. The same guy who had leased to the original owners leased it all together on a preset contract made by the old guard for a ninety-nine-year lease. This meant that they would have to keep the building or vacate the glass palace and all. Our machinery, while still in good shape, was soon to be outdated; this was a point against us. We were an older bunch as well. We might be seen as a liability to the insurance company. In the end, my head said they would get rid of us, and my heart said, "Don't you believe it."

The next day, Gale announced at the supervisors' meeting that she was leaving. She had accepted another job, and the quality control job was vacant. I felt this was another bad sign, as Gale was very smart, and she had decided that rather than go down with the ship, she would leave.

I asked her later what her thoughts were. She said she could not take it anymore. She was going to go and work with special needs children. I asked her if she thought we would close, and she said she did not know, but she had to do this for herself. She warned me at that time, "Don't trust the Mexican." As she was my confidante, I told her that I would always keep him at a distance from me.

Later that day, the Mexican came to my office and tried to put my mind at ease. He then hit me with what his plan would be if there were more store closings. He would shut down gravy altogether, as he saw this area as one that did not compete well with other brands there. He would keep the coffee department, the spice room, the drink mix room, and tea. He would eliminate the spice room supervisor, and I would become plant superintendent with team leads. He would do away with all but two packers to train staffing agency employees, and he would produce about 3.5 million dollars in profit. Then he said if we could get them to go ahead with the government contract, we could grow again.

Now, I don't know if he was trying to convince me to stay or if this was what he really thought he was going to do. I could not tell. This meant my crew would have done as I asked and still lost their jobs. This meant the Mexican's word was no good, but it also meant that mine would be no go as well. I had reasoned that I did not want to live with that. I wanted my promises to be kept. If this time came to pass, I would be struck with a moral issue that I could either keep my job or fight against it. I thought if I was pushed against the wall, I knew what I would do. The only way he could do it without me was by using Dewayne and Red together to take my place. It would be difficult, but it was feasible. I had known them both for over twenty years, and I had taught them both everything I knew.

So, I went to them. I got them together, and we went to the abandoned detergent part of the plant. There was a room that was hard to get to, and we could talk there. I started with "We have known each other for over twenty years and have shared a lot of memories. I have always told you guys the truth and never kept anything the Mexican has said to me from you. If we survive, this is what he intends to do."

I then told them of his plan and what cuts he would make. I told them I could not in good conscience go forward with it, that it was not fair to replace the remaining packers who had done all he and I had asked with temps. I told them if I refused, he would approach them to take my place. It was the only move he could make.

I said, "Now you have a choice if this comes to pass. Either we stand together and protect what is left of the packers, or I go on down the road, and you can live with what he does next. It means that we will not make as much profit, but you are talking half a million dollars versus what I have promised these people."

We agreed that we would stick together; he could not do it without us. This was if we survived. I had my pieces in place, and when the time came, I would play this last round of human chess if it came to it. I had secured my packers without him knowing it. I could at least take some comfort that I had done this. At least it was one worry on my mind that I could let go. I hoped against all odds that I would get to play this card against him because it would mean survival. I had hopes, but my head still told me what I feared was coming would come to pass.

CHAPTER 24

THE NEWS RELEASE

Time eased forward quickly, and before you knew it, Gale's time to leave was almost upon us. She had given a whole month's notice to train someone else. This in turn was her last remaining quality control employee. I was saddened by her leaving, because she had helped me to learn so much in the lean system and about quality control. I had even started doing some of the buyer's jobs in recent weeks. Imagine that the very first job that I was denied, now after twenty-five years, I was doing. She had helped me with that as well as what to look for from a quality-control perspective concerning raw goods.

Then right before her last week, it was leaked from down the street that there would be a news conference the following week. The rumors flew around that this was it, our last roundup. We had all speculated to what we hoped wasn't coming. Then the Mexican told me that he had learned that they had been conducting a cost survey to compare us with other outside companies that wished to take the business from us. He had reasoned, as I did, we could not be undersold. I knew this was now the reason that the government contract had not been pushed through. They were sitting on it until the survey was complete.

This was being done for months, and we had just now learned of it through Gale's counterpart down at headquarters. This either was bad or good; either they found out that we could not be undersold and would keep us, or they would use the roof or something else to get rid of us. I did not sleep for a week. I did not want to believe after twenty-five years that it all was coming down to this. They had said that the new CEO was a pure grocery guy and did not like manufacturing plants. I had hoped that the fact we could produce him profits when the company was losing money would change his mind.

The next week came, and the plant was on edge. The release would come out on Tuesday morning. That morning, I sat with the payroll clerk, and we watched the intercompany website to see what the news release would say. The release would come out at 10:00 a.m., and it was about 9:30 a.m. I then noticed two people I had never seen before carrying briefcases and heading for the Mexican's office. It was a black man and a little blond woman. They went in and closed the door behind them. In about ten minutes, the Mexican came out and came to me. He said for me to gather the spice room supervisor, the mechanics' supervisor, and Gale and find the buyer. He said, "Meet me in the conference room." He was pale.

When we gathered and were all there, the Mexican looked at us and said, "These are my people. I will tell them." He took a deep breath, tears welled in his eyes, and he announced at 9:50 a.m., we would be shutdown. He said, "I am so sorry. I really thought we would survive, and you have all done an outstanding job to keep this place open."

I was flooded with emotions. I asked, "How was this decision made?"

The black man said, "They think it's cheaper to outsource your product."

I responded, "It is impossible to do so."

He said, "This place needs a roof, and that costs money."

Angered, I responded, "They will have to put a roof on this damn place anyway. It's on the same lease as headquarters, and the man won't subdivide it unless one is put on it."

He said, "Look, I am sorry. Their minds are made up."

The Mexican said, "Let it go, Rick."

I said, "Let it go! Twenty-five years of hard work and five years of putting up with bullcrap from your California Boys promising us the moon and giving us this!"

The blonde said, "I know you are upset, but there is nothing that can be done."

Gale put her arm around me, and I struggled to hold back the tears. It had finally happened: my worst fears were realized. My father was right, and the Lord knows I wished he wasn't. If he would have ever been wrong, I wished this was one of those times.

They waited for me to compose myself, and the Mexican sent us to round up the plant and have them meet in the break room. I fought back tears at each department as I rounded up my employees. When Dewayne reached me, he asked, "What's up?"

I told him only that it was bad. We assembled in the break room, and they came in and gave the rest of the plant the bad news. They explained that we were to be shut down and that they had figured it would take sixty days to do so. They said as we decrewed, severance packages would be given out. I thought that the plant was starting to hate me. I had been part of the layoff process and seen a lot of good people to the gate. I had developed an "us against them" way of thinking to save my crew. I thought all along I was doing the right thing, now this.

When the meeting was over, one by one, they came to me and hugged my neck. I was overwhelmed with emotion. They each told me I had given them hope for a long time and that I had fought with every tool I had to keep them alive. I had believed in them and believed we could pull through together.

When Dewayne came, he said something to me that I will always carry. He said to me, "Hold your head up, Rick Johnson!" He explained to me that the general feeling was that I would fight until my last breath for that plant. He said when the plant fell behind in the face of plant closures, I had picked them up and kept moving forward. "Every time someone was down, you grabbed them up and pulled them along. You have carried the burden of this plant on your shoulders and the lives of forty people with you for long enough. You did everything they let you do. The Lord wants you to put it down now."

I hugged his neck, and we cried. It would be as it was with my father, a wound not easily healed.

Perhaps other folks would have said we were too emotional, but we had been through so much. We had implemented the lean system.

We had transformed the plant into a showplace and a shining example as to what a clean food manufacturing plant should look like. We had reached world-class production records with machines that would soon be outdated. We fought, on one front, the largest food manufacturers in the world and had held them at bay. We, our small little band, had done the impossible with limited resources, and all the while, plant closings were falling around us. We lived under so much stress for so long that many of our team had reached the breaking point. In a weird way, it had been held over our heads that we would be closed for so long it was a relief it was over.

Now I waited for what was next. My departments ran faster so we would be out of supplies and materials quicker than the rest. My friend who had asked me to go to our rival coffee company now owned his own business with his father and mom. He assured me I had a job there. So, I proceeded to run my departments out. I threw the last coffee bag into the hole. I roasted the last roast. I ground the last bit of coffee. I ran the last bit out of all our machines and kept the last bag and last cans. I packaged the last cases and stacked the last case on the pallet. I followed suit in the other departments. I inventoried the leftover materials and turned the numbers in. I contacted the congresswoman and told her the bad news. I said if she ever came through again to call me. My wife and I had enjoyed her company, and I told her she was always welcome at my house. I made my arrangements to go on and work with my friend. I did not want a severance package. I was a working man and wanted a paycheck.

The Mexican sat me down, and we had a long talk. He had checked into what it would cost to start our own business. I asked him where the money was coming from; he wanted me, Dewayne, and Red to go in with him. I said I would talk to the boys, but I had not approached them about it. He knew we had retirement accounts, and we could now access them. I knew something else that he did not know: they would not sell us the roasters because of the no-compete policy. And if we started a coffee business, we would be competing with who they were using to make the company brand coffee. There would still be a company coffee; we just would not make it.

I also knew he wanted us three because he could use one of us against the other if he wanted to because we all had about the same knowledge. Dewayne and Red did not trust him. Red went to work at the main warehouse and stayed with the company. Dewayne stayed behind to close the plant and then started looking for a job. His father had enough work for him to do. I told the Mexican if he could float the money out there and if he could find the equipment, I could work for him. I said, "Until then, my friend, it is adios."

I thanked him for all he had taught me and for the things he let me do. When I readied myself to say goodbye to everyone, I told him first before I made my final lap around the plant. I again told him I appreciated him believing in me and letting me fulfill my dreams there. He told me this: "I never let you do anything. You should have been doing these things all along. Rick, you were dealt a terrible injustice here. They had the most talented guy right in front of them all along. But you made yourself so important in the coffee department they wanted to keep you there. They chose to hold you down. They needed to protect the crown. They needed that coffee department and knew you were what was best for running it efficiently. And they knew your love for this place would keep you here. No, I did not *let* Rick Johnson do anything. You was due, my friend."

I thanked him, and he hugged my neck and told me if I needed anything to call him.

I now was about to do what was to this point in my life one of the toughest things I would ever do. I was about to say goodbye to people that I had been around for over twenty years. They saw me grow up, they saw my struggles, and they saw my victories and my losses. They had been with me for the death of my father and through a divorce and had seen me marry the best woman I could have ever met. They accepted her with open arms and made her feel like part of the family. They helped me in my struggles and worked shoulder to shoulder with me. They supported me, and I supported them. I knew that once I said goodbye, many of them I would never see again. You always say you will stay in touch, but you drift apart. I knew this was going to be the case.

Each room was very tough, and I openly wept at saying goodbye. I wished them well. Now Dewayne I knew I would see again. The worst of all was when it came time to say goodbye to Charlie Tree. He had known me longer than anyone. We were hired within a couple of weeks of each other. We had a lot of memories. We had went fishing, crabbing, and many sporting events together. When I went to where he was, when he saw me, he began to cry. He said, "I surely wish this day would have never come. I will tell you this: if anybody could have pulled us out of this, it was you. Nobody else would have even tried."

He grabbed me and put his forehead to mine, and the tears just ran. If you have ever seen a black man and white man behave this way, you would know there does not have to be prejudice in this old world. I loved this man as he loved me, as brothers. He looked up and said, "Stay in touch, you hear." He then said, "I love you, Rick Ranger."

About that time, the Hawk arrived and joined in the crying. When he hugged me, I thought he would squeeze the life out of me. I bid them farewell, and then Charlie Tree did the neatest thing. He went to the loudspeaker and put on a taped version of "Midnight Rider." Big Hawk had gone on the other PA system and as loud as he could shouted, "Rick Ranger has left the building!"

As I went to the truck, I could hear other people joining in. I heard the voices of my family there chanting my name. I stopped to see them gathered at the docks to wave goodbye. I stopped, revved the old Dodge up, and laid on the horn. I left to my theme song. I was gone, and now it was time to write another chapter in the book. I tried to stay in touch with a few, but we sort of drifted apart. Charlie later had a stroke and is disabled. The rest of the crew and I have not been together, except for Dewayne and B. We are still close. Maybe soon though.

CHAPTER 25

IRON AND STEEL

Well, here I was, starting over at forty-five years old. Thankfully, my friend, whom I had been friends with for almost forty years, had a place for me to go. I had been courted by some other plants that had found out I was soon to be out of a job. I had met them at the lean seminars and work classes we had attended. I thought I would give manufacturing a rest now. I refused the offers and went to work with my pal.

I have known him since we were seven. His demeanor is so much like mine. He had been called the Cheshire Cat in school. His grin was always on his face, and it went from ear to ear. And his kindness and attitude toward people were stellar. He lived by the Golden Rule: Do unto others as you wish they would do unto you. Treat people as you wish to be treated. Hard work thrives in him.

To say that I now was a fish out of water would not be correct. Let us say I was more like a frog away from the pond. I figured if I hopped around long enough, I would find my way back. I could find my way in this new line of work. So came the time for me to go talk to Pop. My buddy's dad was one of the toughest fellows you ever want to meet. He was raised in an old-school way and worked hard, as hard could be, his whole life. He was and is an accomplished pilot and chopper copper as well. He was a reserve police officer early on and had taken to being a helicopter pilot for the sheriff's office. He did all this while raising a family and working a full-time job. He continued to do so, as he and his son had started this business. He was like a father to me, and I respected his every word. This was because there was nothing but truth that came from his mouth. And he had known me since I was seven years old. There are few people that you can trust in this old world; he is one of them.

So, I went to sit down and talk to Pop. Pop told me it was late in life for me to be switching professions. He said though it was my buddy's call, and we could work it out. So, I started out driving the trucks. I had a flatbed, a pipe truck, and a utility truck; there were also two work trucks. I delivered finished goods that they created in the shop. They welded and fabricated just about anything made of iron or steel. I also went and picked up materials from our vendors.

I was nervous about this. I had never hauled anything like this stuff before. The bulk of my hauling experience was hauling two-by-fours from the lumberyard. Sometimes I had thousands of pounds of iron and steel on the old flatbed. I, however, was trained by a dude they called the Kevinator. He was a bit younger than me with salt-and-pepper hair close cut. He was built tough and was a good, kind man who spoke softly yet had a toughness that he did not need to show.

He trained me well in material handling, and he went with me on my maiden journeys to the shredder, the steel companies, and the saw-mills. He taught me how to secure loads and how to do rigging, what I could haul, and what I could not. He introduced me to people wher-ever we went, and he made me feel welcome to be with them. Over my time there, he taught me a barrage of things I needed to know. I thank him for that.

My buddy had told me that unlike fellow sophisticates such as he and myself, very often, this line of work drew in the dregs of society. He said many times that they gave jobs to folks with, let's just say, checkered pasts. So, he insisted that other than the Kevinator, Gary, and Chuck to guard my loins.

The guy they had running the crew I believe was one of those guys. The Eagle, as they called him, was a very rough-looking biker dude. He could do anything with iron or steel. He had what they called mad skills. He was tough, and I had even seen him weld his wedding ring to himself. He could cut steel with a torch and do it barehanded. He, however, did not like me. I think it was a combination that I and the boss were so close, and I was totally new to this line of work. I think he resented me, and we butted heads many times. He was unlike any supervisor I had ever had. He did not know how to talk to people. Perhaps his gruff style was due to the people he had worked with be-fore. I tried to just do my job and ignore him. I think the other guys thought I just let him run over me. The reality of the situation was my buddy was under enough stress trying to run the business. There was no sense adding to his worries with arguments he would have to settle. I did not like the Eagle.

We had good old Chuck, who was a finesse welder. He had an altogether different style than the Eagle. Chuck eased his way through things, while the Eagle bullied his way through. They did not get along, and Chuck never agreed with the Eagle's dangerous tactics. Then there was Gary. Gary was a nice dude who just kept his head down and did his job. He was a strong guy, and I liked him well. Gary did not have a checkered past though and is now rebuilding in Iraq.

Now over my time there, just like in my manufacturing days, I saw many kinds of folks. Just about all I met were, I was sure, dependent on some type of substance. They could fool a drug test, but I had been around enough to know a user when I saw one. However, they did not last long, Pop would use them long enough to work them good and hard, and they either quit or were run off. I just kept my mouth shut and did as I was asked to do.

The truck-driving job allowed me a certain freedom I had never had. I was given a list of things to deliver or pick up, and many times, I was gone from early morning until the afternoon. In most cases, my trips took me down country roads to get to town and other places to get supplies and deliver what we had built. I enjoyed early fall mornings with a coffee mug in hand driving the back country roads. This, though, was almost always followed by going into the teeth of traffic to fetch iron sticks and sheets of steel. Winter was good, but on the summer days, it would get hot. A stop in traffic when it's ninety-five degrees and 100 percent humidity can be taxing on a driver with no air-conditioning. Yet it had a sense of freedom to it. I have yet to feel that again.

Most days, I wound up going to what was known as the shredder. This was at the junkyard, and it ate a variety of things. It would chew up cars or buses with ease. It was a dangerous machine, and it would eat you too if you were not careful. When it ran, the ground shook for a hundred feet in all directions. It was a beast, and it was our company's main source of income. We did repairs on it all the time, just so this animal could keep eating cars. On a regular basis, it was breaking welds and twisting shafts. That was our forte. We fixed it and kept it running. This and the sawmills really kept us in business. We did other jobs, but none brought in the cash that the shredder did.

Then it came to pass that we were told that the shredder that was its own company would now be part of the larger mill that was on the same property as it was. That meant we would have to gain a contract with them to be able to work on the shredder. I sensed bad things now. The other part of this company was under new management. I thought that they would start to lean things down. I saw that our company was doing things at the shredder that their own mechanics should be doing. It was plain to see for me. The main guy at the shredder hung on for a while and then was gone.

We did, however, get the contract, and it opened new jobs with the whole company, not just the shredder. So, we expanded, and new help was brought in. The Eagle, though, had his own plans. He had secretly been trying to start his own little company using the contacts Pop had made. He had figured out that if he could get them to slide him just a little of our work, he could do his own thing. He had been taken care of well by our company. He was given a down payment for a house. He was always given a good wage. He was flown home up north when there was a problem with his family. Yet he spoke ill of Pop and my friend and was openly jealous of what they had.

He came in and quit. He struck out on his own. I have no problem with someone wanting to own their own business, but it was the way he went about it. He took jobs from us to get going, and we had been the reason he was there in the first place. What he did not figure on was that his work ethic and how he had come about these jobs did not go unnoticed by the new management. It was not long before he was thrown off the property and told they could not use him there anymore. In the next six months, I would see him more and more coming around the shop. Then one day, they hired him back. In my opinion, he had betrayed my friend, his dad, and the company. He was skilled, but he was not the only one in town who knew how to do what he did. I think it best not to reward people who try to cut your throat. I was just a driver though. What did I know?

Soon something happened to the girl we had in the office, and she was let go. I was then asked if I could learn to do payroll. So, I did. Mom started teaching me the office. I split my time between the office and the road. I learned payroll and how to handle the accounts. I was taught how to bid the jobs on paper and do spreadsheets to show the customers where their money was going. I liked this, and I was now privy to all our business. I knew where the money was coming from and going. I felt at ease doing this but always kept Mom close at hand in case I ran into trouble. I think this did not set well with the Eagle. I now knew more about the company than he ever would. I was trusted, and I always kept my mouth shut about the company business.

Things were good for quite a while. I was making decent money. I had almost every weekend off to spend with my wife and enjoyed that. Then something happened to me. I came down ill. It was like when I had caught pneumonia before. My breathing was not right, and my heartbeat felt funny. I thought I was just getting a bad case of the flu. I went to a doc in the box, and they said my heart was enlarged. I needed to go to my primary doctor. I did, and before I knew what was happening, I was in the cardiac ward at the hospital.

They ran tests and said my arteries were clean, but my heart had jumped rhythmically. They tried to shock me with the paddles to get it back in pace. It did not work. I was put on blood thinners, something to control blood pressure, and something to slow my heart down. Now I was very upset. I had always been in good health and had taken care of myself. The medicine, when taken at night, would make me dizzy the next morning. I tried to get myself used to it. Some days, I would wake up with my head swimming.

I researched my condition and found out that years ago they would have said that I had an irregular heartbeat and let it go at that. But now they had linked this with heart attacks and strokes. I found out that treatments for this condition were new. It had its own classification and line of medicines that were being used largely on an experimental basis. I guess I looked as if it would take a lot to kill me because my doctor wanted to try it all. However, I did not bite on it. He told me if I did not do something, my heart would beat itself to death in ten years. That was seventeen years ago now as I submit this book.

I was told that he was one of the best in the world at treating this condition. I thought I knew my body, and I was the best in the world at that. Each time he suggested a new treatment, I countered it by do-ing my own research to see what the odds of success were. In each case, there was no data to show that there was a permanent fix to it. Yet he pushed everything at me: oblation, more heart shocks with new kinds of medicine, a pacemaker of all things to control my heartbeat.

The oblation was where they went in, found the part of your heart that was acting up, and burned it to kill it. I found it was not a cure and had talked to people who, after having this done, inside a year were right back in there to do it again. The defibrillator paddles did not work either; they were only a temporary fix. A pacemaker was for old folks. I still could control my heart rate with my mind. I wasn't going to take the brain out of the loop. If I let him do these things, I felt as if I would become disabled. I could not continue in the line of work I was in.

He reminded me of a car salesman, pushing one car at me after another to see if I would buy one. I did not let him do anything. I lost about seventy pounds over the course of two years, and most days, I really felt pretty good. On my last visit to him, when he began to insist, I do something, I told him I felt great, and if I started to feel bad, I would do something then. He told me that feeling great was all in my head and that my body had just gotten used to the condition. I fired him on the spot. I got a second opinion and was told that with the medications, we could manage my condition, not cure it. I chose this path.

I continued to work and do the best I could. Most days, I could do my job. What my friend who owned the business did not know was that some days it was a struggle to make it to work and perform my job. The medicine left me washed out, and it was a fight to regain energy. I pushed on, and after a while, I began to get used to the medicine. With enough coffee, I was fine. They continued to work with me, and I did the best job I could.

Then I started seeing a disturbing trend in the business. Things were slowly tapering off. When I made my runs to my vendors, I started to notice that people I had been seeing were not there anymore. When I would ask where they were, I was told things were getting slow, and they had been laid off. The building of things was slowing down. The sawmills went first. When the bottom fell out of the housing market, there were no new houses being built, so there was no new wood needed. I saw our second largest customer go from running around the clock to two shifts and then one shift. With less production, that would mean fewer things breaking and tearing up for us to fix. That also meant less money for outside projects for improvements.

It had started there, and sure enough, it spread to the meat of our business. The steel company went from around the clock to two and then one shift. They began to have our crew come out and teach their guys to do some of the jobs we had been doing. They slowed any outside work being done to a crawl. I saw our profit margin begin to fall. I saw that now we were struggling to make payroll.

I knew what this would mean for me. I had by then done my own matrix, and I was now the weakest player in this game. It was true that I knew how to do many jobs for them, but I did not know how to weld, not like the other guys could. I did not know how to make things from raw steel. I had busied myself with what I thought I could do well for them. On the jobs, I kept them supplied. When cranes were needed, I had learned to do the rigging for lifting objects that it amazed me we were lifting. I used pretty much any pneumatic tool they made. I cleaned up the rough welds with grinders to smooth out what they had made. And many times, I painted them. I could use a torch and cut a straight line or cut off nuts and bolts when need be. I had applied myself in the office and taken care of the business through my driving. I had applied everything I knew about business, and I figured if they stayed strong, there would be a place for me.

I also knew as slow as it was that Mom could come back and run the office, the Kevinator could do the runs, and what was left of the crew could do what other jobs I did. I was going to be eliminated. They bled it as long as they could; we all went for thirty-two hours for a while. Then the day came, and I knew it would. My buddy came and said they would have to lay me off. It hurt him deeply to do so, and even though the Eagle had betrayed them, his mad skills kept him his job. I was told as soon as things turned around, I would be brought back. At first, I thought maybe this would not be so bad. I would be off for a little while and then carry back on. I could get some things done at home and then go back to work. Wrong!

CHAPTER 26

THE LONG ROAD

So here I am, almost fifty, out of work, and starting over again. Like so many of us, I filed for unemployment and began my job search. I thought at first maybe this would not take long. I polished myself a new résumé, contacted some folks, and began to submit applications. I thought it might be a good idea to go back to food manufacturing. I had been a supervisor, and I knew the lean concepts. This would get me a job quick. I had remembered what Pop said about changing lines of work at such a late age. I put my résumé on the job posting sites, and every time there was something remotely matching my skills, I applied.

What I found out that I can pass along is this: when you first post, every staffing agency in town will contact you to do phone interviews. You are a new prospect and might meet what their customers want. I did many phone interviews and found in many cases that the jobs were out of town or had some crazy hours. Still, except for going out of town, I was game. But for the time being, I still wanted to work a day shift.

I was sent by two staffing agencies to the same job interview. This job was at an air-conditioning filter company. They needed a lean manager. I went suit and tie, and I was well prepared. I had done my research on the company. I waited outside as they interviewed the first guy. I paced like a tiger in a cage outside the door, as there was nowhere to sit. When it came my turn, I exploded in the interview. I spouted everything I knew and all I had done that had led me to their door.

I talked about their company and the fine things they had done and all of the things I had accomplished over my thirty-year journey through the working world. My friend, I had just totally awed every bit of the twenty-seven-year-old plant manager sitting in front of me. He, after hearing of my feats, said, "Mr. Johnson, you are what we are looking for. You are the man for this job."

He continued, "Let me bring in my safety supervisor to meet you."

I said, "Sure thing, John," as I called this lad by his first name. He walked out, and I thought, Man, that was easy. I had done a great job. I had been to one interview and nailed it.

Then, the safety supervisor came in, and she was an equally young person of mid- to late twenties. She asked me to tell her about myself, and I went back through the exact thing I had just said before. Then she asked me about safety. I went on and on. I could see though the more I knew about it, the more uncomfortable she became. At times, I looked to the plant manager and back to her. I could read that he was thinking, Why doesn't she know about these things? Also, why did she not know the procedures that go with them? I asked if their supervisors did safety audits, and she looked as if she would faint. I then looked at him, and he was wondering the same thing. She was totally intimidated by me, and I could sense it. I hushed in an attempt to end the interview. It had worked, but now I had a bad feeling. I asked when they would decide on this, and I was told soon.

I left feeling like I had done a good job, but now I felt, maybe I did too good a job? I knew I had made the safety supervisor look bad. How was I to know that she did not know what she should have? Days went by, and I finally contacted the staffing agency and asked what the status was on the job. They told me they had decided not to hire for that position; they instead promoted someone inside. I was told that I would be contacted when another job came up matching my job skills.

Now that was my first taste of rejection. I had learned what I should have already known. Don't intimidate the hiring people. I came on too strong. I had lost the job when she walked in the room, and I knew more about her job than she did. I had learned that the staffing companies will lie to you also. They want their cut of the pie. You are a product for them to sell, and if you don't fit, they will gladly sell them another. Upon doing my research about them, I found that you had to sign a contract for ninety days, and at that point, they could keep you another ninety days if they decided to. This is what most do, so they are paid for your efforts.

So, I settled back into the same routine. Every morning, I found myself on the computer from seven until noon, digging and searching for a job. I would find something that looked good and write cover letter after cover letter. I would tailor my résumé to the job and hope for the best. Using key words in the actual job description as to what they were looking for gets you past the computer. What I realized was happening was that more and more folks were losing their jobs.

As more folks lost their jobs, the job market was getting tighter. The jobs that I would have been suited for now required the degree I had not obtained. I guess I should have listened to the human resource guy a long time ago. Now, at almost fifty years of age, I could not see going back to school. I pressed onward in my search, and even jobs that required a degree I would apply to. I tried to make them see that all my years in manufacturing would outweigh a two-year degree. I beat my head against that wall for a long time.

What I was competing against was this. I live in a town of roughly a million folks. Out of those million, let us say half are in the workforce. The rest are children or old folks. That means maybe five hundred thousand are in the workforce. Unemployment had now reached 10 percent. That meant that fifty thousand of us were looking for work. I had seen that in our town maybe fifty new jobs came up a day. That meant that 49,950 of us would not be hired that day. Not only that, maybe twenty or so more were losing their jobs that day. So, you see what all of us were up against.

Let us add in some other factors now. They say the age factor does not play a role here. That is just not true. Hiring managers are not supposed to discriminate and ask your age. They don't have to; your résumé will tell it all. When they look at your work history, they should be able to ascertain your age. Some require when you graduated school; that tells your age right there. Now add about fifty or sixty pounds to your frame. You are also at the age that you are turning gray as well. Your package does not look as good as the knowledge that is in it. You are a liability to a company now. Ask yourself if you were selling life insurance, whom would you gamble on, the fifty-year-old person carrying extra pounds or the just-out-of-college person in their twenties? I will get back to the life insurance later. If this is not true, why are these ads on television for getting the gray out of your hair before the big interview? I even saw one for a body-slimming suit so you looked trimmer for the big job interview. These things do matter, and your knowledge for all intents and purposes is secondary.

They are afraid you won't have that fire that a younger candidate would have. Or soon you would be a burden to their insurance company. I fell into this category. I was older; I had now started to put on more weight because I was not moving around as much. Over the years, my hair started to get that gray in the temples look.

I had been hard on my body physically. Not all work-related injuries, but I had some resume on the injury list. I had obtained one hell of a concussion from a truck crash. It bothered me for months afterward. I tore my rotator cuff in my shoulder, which left me to do my job with one arm for six weeks. That was my last sandlot football game. It still gets sore. I had separated six, seven, and eight of my ribs lifting weights. That took a month to heal, and when it gets good and cold, they remind me of it. The worst was I had separated my right bicep trying to catch a falling roaster pipe. I was told there was nothing that could be done for it. That pretty much slowed my weightlifting down. I had broken my right thumb, and my ankles had suffered greatly over the years. I tore the ligaments in my ankles over and over and finally broke my left one, but the one on the right hurts worse. So, yes, I have been banged up pretty good over the years, and now my heart was out of rhythm to boot. So now here is the question: Could I still bring the heat? Could I summon the fire within me to go out and aggressively do a job?

You see, if you're in the manufacturing world, as I clarified very early on, speed is the key. You must be able to keep up with the machines. If I could not land a management job, I would have to go for an operator. If this was the case, I would have to move and move fast to please the boss. I knew this going in, but I still was going to shoot for management. I had to keep trying for these jobs even though I knew my chances were slim to none without the degree.

So, I kept at it, and time began to drift on. I would go on doing what I was doing. After a month or so, I received another call from another staffing agency. They said there was a company that produced bulletproof vests that was looking for a supervisor. The job was day shift and a worthy cause as well. I went for the interview, and I met directly with the plant manager. It was not a sit-down interview. He conducted it as he showed me around the place. I found some stuff as we were walking around that would improve his process. We connected, and I felt pretty good about our conversation. At the end, he told me that this was a contract job, and that inside a year, they may or may not have the contract. That meant he may or may not have work for me in a year. I needed a job, so I said that I understood and would still be happy to take the job. He said good and that he had to hash some things out with the staffing agency, and we could go from there. I thanked him for his time, told him what a wonderful thing they were doing, and bid him adieu.

About three days went by and no word. I called the staffing agency to follow up. I was told they wanted me, but there was a holdup on their end. I asked how long it would take for this to be resolved. She didn't know. She assured me that when she knew she would contact me and for me to hang on.

Two weeks went by, and I received another phone call from them. They wanted a second interview. I went, and the human resource girl said to me that the shipping supervisor wanted to talk to me. She then said that when he saw my résumé he had asked her if he could talk to me. When I met him, we went to his office, and he asked me if I had a copy of my résumé, as he had not seen it. The human resource girl had lied to me. He had not seen my résumé, and now I wondered why she said what she said. Why lie about it? All I could figure was that she was trying to keep me interested in this place.

He asked some questions and gave me a tour of their shipping office and area. It was small, and I thought it looked very manageable. He told me who would be training me and what it involved. He asked when I could start, and I told him as soon as they needed me. He said that it would be soon, but there were some things that needed hashed out. I said okay, and he sent me back to the human resource girl.

She then began her own interview. Now I did not trust her. I had caught her in a lie. I, however, reacted well and gave my spiel. She asked all the questions out of the interviewer's handbook. I answered well and saw that with each answer it was the response she wanted. At the end, I had answered one question I felt was wrong. When asked what I would do with an employee who had a problem in performance, I said that I would try to coach them and handle it internally, and then if that did not work, corrective actions would follow. She did not like the answer.

I think by looking at her, she thought human resources should become involved right away. I had been taught to handle every problem I could on the floor and not on the carpet. It saved managers headaches and made your employees respect you more. It would keep write-ups out of their personnel files. I was told they would contact me soon, but once again, there was something that needed hashed out.

I did not know what needed to be hashed out, but I was wishing they would do it. Two weeks went by and nothing. I contacted the staffing agency again, and I was told there was a holdup in negotiations for that vest company's contract. They were waiting for an answer to see if they would get the contract. I was told as soon as they did, I would be hired, and as soon as they knew something, I would be contacted. By this time, I had over a month tied up in this and no answers. It did not matter, as I was not getting any other calls anyway. There was, however, one thing pushing me. I needed insurance.

I had the snake package. You know the one you get when you get laid off. This plan costs as much as your unemployment check gives you. If you have a preexisting condition, you cannot find insurance anywhere. They are aware of this and take full advantage of it. Now the government did give me some relief through a bill they passed to ease the pain. It did cut it in half, and it would now only cost me one of my checks to keep it. My new condition required monthly lab visits to keep my rat poison dose safe. Warfarin, which is what I am on, is used in rat poison. It has to be monitored regularly. I would only go to the doctor if I had to. But when the relief package ended, my insurance went to three of my checks. When I called and asked if there was a mistake, I was told no. I asked if they realized that this package was supposed to be for people who were laid off. I was told yes by the lady on the other end of the line. I then asked if the insurance company knew that unemployment pay was roughly a thousand a month, and they want almost nine hundred for insurance. I asked, "What do you think I will do, be insured or eat?"

I was promptly told that was the way it was, and I could seek insurance elsewhere if I liked. I could not find anyone I had ever heard of to insure me.

A job with benefits was what I was after. Every day, the search continued as I awaited a call from the vest company. I was still waiting for them to hash out whatever it was they were trying to hash out.

Then I saw an ad for a material handler, and it sort of dealt with some of the stuff that I did for my buddy. It had said they had opened an on-site shop at a local steel company. It had to be the one that I used to deliver to. I sent a résumé and a cover letter and received a call. It was at the place I thought it was, and I knew just about everybody there. The company was, however, new to them and had just opened this on-site shop. The pay for the job was good, better then when I was a supervisor. I agreed to meet with them on a Tuesday morning for the interview at a local hotel.

Well, as fate would have it, the vest company called the Friday before and wanted me to come in the same day, first thing in the morning, for yet another interview. I had already made two trips to this place and had been given the runaround. I asked the staffing person point-blank what had been the holdup. I was told that they wanted to hire, but the contract was not in place. I then asked, "Is it in place now?"

She replied, "Well, no, but they are close."

I then asked, "Why was I being sent for another interview and not being hired?"

The response was slow in coming, and I did not trust them. I was then told this was just the last step in their process.

I was not going to toss the interview for the job paying fifteen thousand dollars more a year for yet another interview with the vest company. I told her that I could come that afternoon but not that morning.

She said, "No, I don't think that will work. They want to see you that morning."

I said, "You will have to talk to them and tell them this, if they want to hire me, then I will be there. I want to know before I leave the house I am hired. They know everything there is to know about me. Other than that, if it is just another interview, I can see them Tuesday evening."

She said, "I will call them and see what they say."

I said, "Please call me when you know something."

I received no call back that day. I think it was their intent to keep me hanging on through interviews until something broke. I am not sure. I focused on researching the other company for the next interview.

The morning came, and I was up bright and early. Showered and shaved with my best suit on, briefcase in hand, I was as prepared as I could be. I entered the hotel, and the man at the desk asked if I was Richard Johnson. I told him I was, and he said that the three men sitting at the table having coffee were waiting for me.

One got up from his chair and approached me. He was a thirty-year-old fellow, maybe, with a mustache and goatee. He had on a pullover shirt, jeans, and tennis shoes. I noticed his counterparts were dressed the same, more like they were going to shoot pool rather than conduct a job interview.

He shook my hand and said, "I am Bob. We spoke on the phone. Come on over. We are having coffee until the interview room opens. You really did not need to dress up like this."

I said, "Well, I thought it better to overdress than to underdress."

With that, we went over, and I introduced myself to the other guys. They were talking about football. I fell right in and talked about football too. I thought, This is good; I am establishing a dialog right away.

After some time, the room opened, and I was asked to come on back for the interview to begin.

Bob again mentioned I didn't need to dress up the way I did. I dressed for a professional interview. This was the way I was taught. The interview itself went much as the others did. I gave my spiel and included that I had worked out at the steel company and was familiar with the plant and the people who worked there. I dropped names of the people I knew and what I had done for them. I figured this would be a leg up since I already knew the people that they wanted me to work with.

Then I was asked if I was familiar with their safety program. I said yes, and I knew the safety director there. My wife had worked with this guy at her old company. I then said, "As a matter of fact, I have my safety badge from there on me."

The man across the desk said, "Let's see it. I want to see what you really look like, not the guy in front of me in the suit."

I handed it across the table and then asked, "How do you know that I don't wear a suit quite often?"

He said, "If you do, you won't work for us."

This guy must have had something against a suit and tie. That was the third comment about the way I was dressed.

Then he said some things I did not like. He wanted to know why our little company was not working out there any more than we were. I told him, "If you go out there enough, you can see what has happened to the workforce and how people have been laid off. Less production meant less our little company could do."

He then tried to indicate maybe we did not do a good enough job for them.

I said, "That was not the case. They were always satisfied with our work." I was starting to get irritated at what he was implying. So, I began my own line of questions. I asked, "Is your company on a yearly contract?"

He said, "Yes."

I then asked, "When did they sign on to be working on site?"

He answered, "It was just recently, in the last few months."

I continued, "Then you have nine months left on your contract?"

He said that they did but that he just knew they would renew it at the end of nine months.

I asked then what made him so sure they would.

He went on saying that they provided a quality service, and theirs was not the cheapest bid, just the best."

I asked him, "Did they ask questions on installation of your product and for SOPs on handling and storage of the product?"

He told me, "Yes, they did."

I further asked, "Have they made you give them instructions in writing? How about pictures of the installation process?"

He said, "Yes. Why do you ask?"

I then said, "I have seen them do the same thing with our company. It is a management tool to begin to do things internally rather than outsource. They are under new management, and as new management, they must save more money. Times are getting hard. It will be easier in the future for them to buy the product from a cheaper source and then use your SOPs to have their guys do the installation."

A very long face came over my interviewer. This, friend, was at the end of the interview. I was told they would be in touch, and that was that.

I am sorry I just could not let this guy act as if it was something my company had done that had caused our cutbacks. The truth of the matter was it was the times we were living in. I think by what he was saying, he was attempting to convince his comrades that what had happened to us would not happen to them. I found out through my buddy who was still doing jobs for the steel company that nine months later, they were gone.

I blew the interview, but the job would not have lasted nine months anyway. I could not have relocated to their other sites. When I came back home, I called the staffing agency and asked what they said at the vest company. I was told they would get back with me. The bird in the hand thing comes to mind. I had cut that line off for another chance. I still don't know if the third interview would have seen me hired or not. Lesson learned: ask about the attire for the interview.

It was back to the drawing board. I kept trying every day. In the meantime, I cleaned house, washed clothes, cooked, and did the yard work. Now it was a long time before I would be given a call for another interview. Months passed by, and I began to write and finish a novel that I had started long ago. So, after my morning job search, I would sit down and write. I found that I really loved to write and wished there was a way to make a living out of it. I still needed a paying job. I would search out every opportunity in town that I could find. It would only take about three hours a day to check on anything new that would come up in our city.

In the meantime, I would get offers over the internet. Most jobs there were for selling insurance. I had considered it, but they were all based off commission. They all sounded good enough, but you must realize one thing: everyone who was posting résumés was getting these offers. It did not matter what your background was, you received them.

Now ask yourself a question. When you go to sell these policies, you cannot very well sell one unless you have bought one yourself, could you? I mean, you must show some faith in your product, correct? So by offering you the job, they, in effect, have sold at least one new policy. Maybe some of your family would buy these polices too. They might get a dozen or more out of you before you cannot meet your quota. Then, it was "See you later." Then they sold some policies, and maybe you got a little in return. Pretty good insurance idea they had there. So, I chose not to pursue that avenue.

Then after some time, I went to another interview to be a supervisor at a huge warehouse. This was one of those deals where this pallet company had a little office at the warehouse and took care of all their pallets. I had done pallet sorting and run crews to do it before. You just put the good ones back into circulation, and the bad ones needed to be loaded back in the trucks to be sent off for repairs. They wanted a person to run it, work a split shift, and get this done with a crew of about ten. The volume of the pallets would be huge. This was the largest warehouse distribution center in our neck of the woods.

This fellow asked me to meet him in the parking lot at the center of the visitor parking area. I was there early and waited and waited and waited some more. After he did not show and was thirty minutes late, I called him. I thought I was maybe at the wrong spot or something. He did not answer. Then about two minutes later, he called back and said he was sorry he was running late. He was staying at a local hotel about fifteen minutes away and would be there soon. I am pretty sure my call awakened this guy.

He finally showed up thirty minutes later. I had been there waiting for over an hour. What else was I going to do? It was not like I had somewhere else to be that day. He met me at the gate, and we went inside. We talked as we walked, and the walk was a long one to the back of the warehouse. After gaining some weight and not being used to walking in the heat, I began to sweat. It was summertime, and it was about ninety degrees and humid. By the time we arrived at their little office, I was huffing a little. Their little office was a desk pushed up against the wall with a computer on it. The work was being done in the parking lot on the concrete. I was escorted outside to see what they did. These folks were suffering.

The heat radiated off the concrete in waves. They worked directly in the sun, and as they sorted, one fellow rode the forklift. They sorted plastic shipping crates as well. I asked this fellow why with the company being so large they could not provide a canvas shelter for these folks to work under. If you are from the South, you know what a little shade can do for some relief from the heat. I saw where this could have easily been done. He did not reply right away. I then asked where they worked when it rained. I followed with, in Florida, it rained almost every afternoon in the summer. He said they did not work. I asked, "Can they not make a place inside here for you to work so you can keep going?"

It was then explained to me that as of late they were not in the company's good graces because the old supervisor had made them mad. He showed me an air-conditioned room that was theirs and was taken away by the management of the warehouse company. It was now just a place for their employees to hang out. This did not look good. He said, "That is where you come in. We need someone to repair our relationship with the company here."

I wiped sweat from my face and said I could do it. I knew, though, that visibly I did not look so good. I was still huffing and puffing from the walk, and my clothes were now wet from the heat. He asked me what I thought about the forklift driver and if we needed to get rid of him.

I replied, "I don't know. I have only seen him work for ten minutes."

He asked me a few more questions, and we started the walk back. We walked, and I tried to talk.

I was mad at myself for being heavier and not walking more. I was having a hard time trying to talk to this guy and walk as fast as he walked. I was just short of being out of breath to the point of stopping for a second to regain my composure. When we arrived at the front of the warehouse, he asked what I thought. I said I was ready to give it a try. He replied he had another interview that afternoon, and it was between me and another fellow. He would let me know. I said I appreciated his time and looked forward to working with him. With that, I headed across the parking lot to my car. When I looked back, I saw he had his head in his hand and was thinking deeply. I am sure that he thought physically I could not perform the job.

On the drive home, I was very upset with myself. For the first time in my job hunt, I felt as if maybe I would not get hired at all. I had let myself get out of shape, and it had definitely hurt me in this interview. I began to wonder what had happened to me. I went from being a supervisor, to truck driving, to now looking for anything to help pay the bills. How had this happened? When did I wake up and realize I was getting to be a middle-aged person? I knew I would not be called for this job. To make matters worse, it was a terrible job to have. Still, I was hurt not to have landed it. The working conditions and the split shift were not things I wanted. When did this happen? I was now ready to accept a job that conflicted with my home life.

The one thing I did not want was to be away from my wife. I did not mind work, but I did not want to see myself at work when she was at home and vice versa. This I felt had caused me to get one divorce.

I knew that my relationship with my wife now was ten times stronger than the one I had had with my previous wife. I did not want to be away from her. Life is so short and a fleeting thing that moments wasted in pursuit of money instead of being with your loved ones and family are moments lost. Memories are lost, and time drifts on and on. I wanted my home life intact. Now though I felt pressure to get a job to help and get benefits. My wife was working right on, and I felt very guilty that she was still getting up and going to work every day while I was at home doing chores. This compounded my doubt in myself.

Was it now true that I was lost to my age and size and not a marketable product? I started to really get down on myself. I tried getting in better shape, but no matter what, the weight stayed on. It was not the same as when I was a kid. The weight was now stubborn. I used to whip myself into shape inside a month. Try as I might, nothing would replace being active for ten or eleven hours of the day. When I was handling the iron and steel, it kept me in good shape. As the days went by, I starved myself and tried to stay busy. I wound up dehydrated and in the hospital for a day for my efforts. Still the weight stayed on. I did, however, feel as if as I walked more, my wind became better. I hoped to be ready when the next interview came about.

Where was I going? What was happening? I thought in the beginning my buddy's business would recover within a year, but it did not. I stayed in touch weekly to no avail. Once during one of our phone conversations, he had said it was getting better. Was I ready to come back to work? I said yes, and he said he was waiting on the word from Pop that they could bring me back. However, the work they had lined up fell through. It was a false bottom my buddy was looking at. Now I was receiving nothing again, no phone calls. I began to think I would have to start living off of my retirement money soon. I knew a lot of folks out there were already doing this. I had been lucky so far and had not had to dip into it, except for insurance payments, which were tax deductible at the end of the year.

As days passed into weeks, I felt more and more down on myself. I even began to wonder if I was that good at what I was doing before. Was I as good at management as I thought? Was I as good as I thought, period? If I was, why were the people interviewing me not seeing it? I started to feel as if I had been lucky when I landed the coffee plant job. Was it that I was in that little world so long that I dominated it from sheer time there? Now pushed out in the open, I doubted my skills. I was feeling as if all I had done before was just a twist of fate. Why had I not pursued a degree? I had many questions of myself, and now at almost fifty years of age and out of work, the answers were not coming to me.

The gloom of the situation would seem to set down on me some days, and I could not drag myself out of it. The writing helped. I had an escape there. Yet many days, I was frustrated at my efforts to land a job to the point where I felt like, "What is the use?" Résumé after résumé, cover letter after cover letter, I had written so much it was all a blur to me. The online sites to help you land a job had different ideas on how to land one every month. Some sites would say one thing one month and be in direct conflict with what they said the next month. The schools advertised daily and wanted you to sign up. Many sites that you would go to in search of a job would have you go through several refusals of schooling first.

The scams that were out there were numerous. They were set up to take advantage of people like me also frustrated at the job search and getting desperate for money. The work-at-home deals and secret shoppers and go to school for free all had hooks in them. Every time I researched one, I found it not to be what it said it was.

A lot of the schools could get you grant money but then require you take another course to get the rest of the degree, and that would come from your own pocket. Where was the money supposed to come from? There were sales jobs, and they all promised you a good salary based on commission. If you ventured out there, you might earn a living or not. The cards would be stacked in their favor to make them money, and maybe you could get a little bit too.

I had already thought this would be my plan B. If my unemployment ran out before I could land a real job, I would have to take one of these jobs and hope for the best. I was devoting all my time to finding a job with benefits and living off the unemployment checks. I was approaching the end of my snake package, and I could not afford the insurance. Something needed to happen and happen soon.

Sometime later, I received another phone call. I had applied for a lead driver position with a parcel company. I did know our city well and had told them in the cover letter that I knew every mile of back road and every inch of railroad track. I did know it all well through driving with my buddy's company and from growing up in the town. I quickly agreed to the interview and was to meet them the next morning at 10:30 a.m. Upon arriving there at 10:15 a.m., I went inside and approached the front desk. I rang a bell that brought someone to speak to me. This middle-aged fellow who I was guessing from his name was of Cuban descent approached me. I introduced myself and told him why I was there. His name was Juan. He asked me if I would mind coming back around 10:45 a.m. I asked if there was a problem. He said they were running a little behind. I said alright and that I would go up the road and get a soda.

I drove around and drank my soda, being careful not spill any on the brand-new shirt I had purchased for just such an occasion. This place was close to the airport, and I looked at all the new businesses out there and wondered if any of them still needed somebody. After about twenty minutes, I went back. I was greeted by no one. I waited until 10:45 a.m. and rang the bell again.

Juan came out and asked me to sit down. They were almost through. I said okay, and he was gone for maybe ten minutes and came back. He apologized for the wait and began to tell me a little about the company. He said they were almost ready to interview me and he would be right back. Ten more minutes went by, and a young fellow came out, escorted by a huge black dude. This guy was the first interview. He was a young guy dressed in a T-shirt and blue jeans. The black guy introduced himself to me as Clinton and asked me to come inside. I went back inside, and there were Juan, and an early thirtyish white fellow named Bill, all of them dressed in a suit and tie.

They apologized for the wait; it was now almost 11:30 a.m. So, I reached into my briefcase and handed them all a résumé saying I did not know if they had a hard copy. They were all staring at their laptops. Bill said that he would tell me a little about their company. He said that they had recently diversified the company into six parts. I had heard that they could not compete against the larger companies.

They had their niche though. They had their hands in all kinds of stuff. This guy went on for an hour about his company. During this time, Clinton kept getting calls and would have to leave. The whole time, Juan just stared at me, reading my emotions.

Finally, Bill quit talking about his company and said, "Tell me what brings you here."

I did as he asked and went into my spiel. The whole time, the Juan guy was staring at me. He was searching for untruths or something in my actions that would indicate I had embellished on something. I had not.

When I was finished, Bill said, "Okay, I am going to go through your résumé. Let me ask you about it." He first wanted to know why I had it written the way it was. I had my coffee plant on there first because that was where I had spent most of my career. He told me for future reference, I should put the last first. I knew this, but most of the people I was sending the résumé to needed to see that first.

He proceeded to go line by line of my résumé and ask me questions about each statement. All the while, Juan watched me like a hawk. I answered flawlessly. I knew my stuff, and everything on that résumé was something I had done. When he was done reading and questioning me about each line of the first part, he asked me this: "Why with all your training with the grocery chain would they let you go?"

I thought to myself the answer was obvious if you read the papers. I told him that the grocery chain had filed chapter 11, and when they shut down the manufacturing plants, the stores, and the warehouses, there was nowhere to go. I explained that a company of 180,000 was now about 150,000. The only jobs being offered were to the mechanics and only a few with A-class certification. He then said he guessed that was why I had left to work with my buddy's company. I did not like where he was heading with all this. He was suggesting that maybe the company wasn't satisfied with me. This made me angry, but I kept my cool.

After questioning me about everything I did at my buddy's company, he then asked me why they would let me go if I did such a good job for them. I told him that it was because I was not fully trained in industrial repair. I couldn't weld too well, nor was I a machinist. He then wanted to know why I had not learned to weld. I told him I could weld some, but they chose to aim me at the business side of things, so that was where I applied myself. Before he could ask me again; I told him that Mom came back to run the office. To keep the business alive, they would have to keep only the family and two people. I knew that he would ask, so I also told him, "You may contact my former employer, and they will verify what I have just said."

Clinton, who had been in and out of the room the whole time, reentered for about the fifth time. He took a seat, and Bill asked, "Let me ask you this. What is your biggest regret in business?"

What I would love to have told him was that I was having to sit there in front of an arrogant smug guy such as he who was just fortunate to have a job right then. But I did not; I told him that it would be that I did not retire from the coffee company.

He was satisfied with that answer. He asked the other fellows if they had anything to add. Juan asked where I thought I would be in five years. Now, in a normal economy, that might be a good question to ask but not in this one. I still gave the answer they wanted to hear, which was the standard answer: part of a team where I could continue to grow and add value to the company. He was satisfied with that. On to Clinton. He looked at me for a long while. He was stumped as to what to ask me. He had not been in the room long enough to hear enough information to ask me anything.

He finally asked me this: "We have kept you here or riding around for almost three hours, yet you seem as cool as you can be. Most people would be upset right about now. How do you explain that?"

I said, "I have dealt with all kinds of situations over my career, and over time, I have learned to be quite patient with my employers and employees." But the real answer was "You are hanging a carrot in front of my nose, and if I want it, I have to stay cool."

Well, that was the end of the interview, and they told me they would decide real soon. It was now 1:15 p.m., and I had been there for three hours.

When I shook their hands and went to leave, Bill asked, "Where is the other interview?"

Clinton said, "He left."

Bill just laughed and said, "Well, let's go to lunch."

I thought to myself as I was leaving that I really needed a job, but this guy would be terrible to work for. How inconsiderate could you be? They had scheduled the interviews to be an hour apart and did not care about the time of the people that they were interviewing. They had a "we don't care" attitude. That may have been the first time that I received that "I have something you want, and if you want it, you're going to put up with whatever I do" attitude. It left a sour taste in my mouth. I thought it was disrespectful to the people out there looking for a job. This job also had no benefits at all to it: no insurance, 401(k), nothing. It was just a $12.00-an-hour job. But it was a job I would have to take if offered to me. As it turned out, it was not.

I had given a perfect interview, no wrong answers, no flaws in my delivery. I wish I could have spoken to them just once more though. I would have told the arrogant interviewers in the future not to spend over an hour telling somebody about your company. Wait and see if it is someone you want to hire. Why spend that much time telling a person about your company if you conduct the interview and see that it is not someone you wish to hire? I am already sold on your company, or I would not be ready to accept a job with you. In this economy, if a person shows up to the interview, they need the job, period. Nothing you can say is going to deter them from wanting the job. Perhaps three or four years ago, selling your company to a potential new hire was necessary, not now. Just to get to the interview is a major accomplishment.

Still no luck. I was not hired again. I was reminded of something the Mexican had told me. If you get to the interview, the job is yours to lose. Perhaps he was right. I did not know, as there was so much competition out there now. I felt bad about it again, that I had lost out on yet another chance at a job. And once again, I knew that I would not have liked working for the people that I was going to be hired by.

What ever happened to be doing something you love to do, and you never work a day of your life? I suppose that it was just a dream that maybe one day my hope would turn into reality. Is it possible to do that? I know so many people who do not.

Most folks I know complain about their jobs and hate them but do the work to pay the bills. It is sort of the way it is for many of us. Now with things like they were, it had to be close to what people dealt with in the Depression era. You would have to take what you could and be happy to get it.

I kept at it, telling myself somebody had to hire me sooner or later. I had resigned myself, if the unemployment ran out, to living off the retirement money and working off of commission somewhere until things changed. I applied to anything now that I thought I could do. I knew there was a chance that I might go do day labor somewhere. I used to hear people say, "Rather than give them a check, let them dig ditches." That is something at fifty years old you don't want to do. But even that would not matter; those jobs went to the illegal immigrants who worked for little or nothing. You could not even get a job doing that.

By this time, my job search was approaching seventeen months, and I was, to say the very least, frustrated. The worst of it was the rejection time after time. You feel so inept, and when you go to an interview, you come across as begging. How could you not come across that way? Each time you go and are not hired, you get a little more desperate about the situation. Each time you are trying not to project that desperation. However, it is still there. You know that the clock is ticking, and what's worse, so does the interviewer.

When they look at your résumé, they see how long you have been off. They may ask themselves the question: why has someone not hired him? If no one else wants him, why should we? I have been asked the question as to how many interviews I'd been on. What is the purpose of that question? Was there a reason that the other hiring managers would not hire me? Did they see something in my interview that this hiring manager did not see? These are questions of doubt that you begin to ask yourself.

They also know that if you have been off a long time, your resources are running low. You have no bargaining power. You cannot dicker over money or benefits. All you can do is sit there and take what they give you—that is, if you are lucky enough to get it.

One day, the phone rang, and a man on the other end of the line asked if I was working yet. I said, "No, not as of yet. What might you have for me?"

He said that he was looking for a quality control guy for a meat-packing plant, and it looked as if I had a lot of food and beverage experience. I told him I had, and he set up an interview. He said that they were looking for a mature person for this job. He said, "I regret to say that the pay is only $10.00 an hour."

I said, "That's okay. Tell me where to go."

He did, and it really was not far from home. I showed up the next day and was met by an older man who worked for the staffing agency.

We went upstairs to an office that had junk piled everywhere. I was surprised at the mess. It was the plant manager's office we were in, and he joined us shortly. After the standard greetings, we went into the interview. I had changed a few things in my delivery and tried to sound more confident. After his questions and my spiel, he looked across the table at me and said, "I want you; I just don't know where to put you. I need a shipping supervisor and a QC guy. I think you would be suited for either. Let me get my current shipping supervisor up here, and he can talk to you a little."

I thought, Okay, this is good. The pay was not, but it sounded as if I was hired.

The shipping supervisor came up, and we left the plant manager's office and went to the staffing guy's office. The shipping supervisor left and said he would be right back; he had something on the dock to take care of. While he was gone, the staffing guy and I talked. He was in his late fifties, and he told me his story about his job search and what he had been through. It seemed as if he had been a manager at a large hotel, and they had closed the hotel that he had been at for many years. He then found himself without a job, and he was off for two years. He had taken the job at the staffing agency for $10.00 an hour. He said that at one time he had been making $70,000.00 a year. I could relate, and we talked about the way things were out in the job search world.

It was not long, and the shipping supervisor came back and said to me, "I have never interviewed anyone before. Before I did this, I was a furniture salesman, so I never have had much of a chance to conduct interviews. I guess you should tell me about yourself."

I went through my spiel, and as I did, I saw that the more I knew about food manufacturing, the less he liked it. I tried to tone it down, but I was getting the feeling that I did in the very first interview I went on. I knew way more about food, food safety, and food production than this guy ever would. He told me that the reason they wanted a shipping supervisor was he was supposed to move up. The interview ended with the staffing agency guy telling me we should hire in about seven days. Now, once again, the plant manager had told me he wanted me, but I was afraid that the supervisor was put off by what I knew.

Seven days came and went, and I did not receive a call. I contacted the staffing guy, and he said they had not told him to go ahead with the hiring process. He said he would call me, and when he did, it was bad news. He said they had decided not to go ahead with the hiring just yet; it would be a while. He then said to me, "I should not tell you this, but I will. The shipping supervisor is rooting against you. He has told the plant manager that if you are hired, you will be gone as soon as a better-paying job comes along, because you had too much knowledge." He then told me that he was afraid that I would take his spot, and that was why he was trying to keep me from being hired. Here it was again. I felt at this point, "What do I have to do to get a job?"

At some of my interviews, I felt as if my size and age were holding me back, and now it was my knowledge of the job. I did not know which way to turn. I started thinking about running my own business maybe. I did not know what I would go into. The service industry came to mind. Maybe I could run a crew of guys doing yard work or a crew of maids doing housework. From years of doing both, I knew how to do these things well, and with my management skills, maybe I could make it work. Then I thought that would be an all-the-time job—no benefits, no retirement other than what I could make. You would have to insure your workers as well. That would take time to develop. You also would need a customer base while you grew the business. This was probably not a good idea for my situation.

CHAPTER 27

THE WAY HOME

It had seemed that all my efforts and all my résumés and cover letters were for naught. My interviews, although I thought they were as perfect as I could give, did not land me a job. I had poured over my résumé and made it as well written as I could. I had bought bigger clothes and cut my hair tight to conceal as much gray as possible. Still, work eluded me. So, I had given in to the idea I would take a softer approach and start doing what I had not wanted to do. My unemployment had all but run out. I think I had one more extension left, if they passed it down from the government, but it was unsure.

I had used up my old snake package and was searching for an insurance company that would insure me and pay the bill when it came to them. That was unsure as well. I had fought off the wolves so far, with my wife and me juggling bills that needed to be paid. We had done well though, and unlike a lot of people, we were prepared for what had happened. We did not know it would take as long as it did to find me work. It was now almost eighteen months.

One day, as I scanned over the usual sites to find work, I came across an ad for a production worker. Food and beverage and lean manufacturing knowledge was desired as well. It did not go into much detail about which company it was or where it was located. I figured it was a close match though and submitted my résumé and a short, unassuming cover letter. One thing I saw but did not care for was it said the job was for second or third shift. It was go time now though, so what I wanted for a shift and what I would take were two different things. I submitted it and went on searching.

My wife came home with an ad in the paper, and it was the same as the one online. The only difference was that it said where they wanted people to go to put in applications or give résumés. It was not far from the house, but I knew there would be a thousand people there. It had also given a fax number so you could fax in your résumé. I sent one with my wife to work, and she faxed it for me. I went on about my search and my chores for another week and a half. Then the phone rang again.

It was a staffing agency, and it was about the résumé for the food and beverage job. I was given a short interview and asked if I could come in two days later at 10:30 a.m. I agreed and thought to myself, I must do something different. At this point though, what could I do differently? I did not know. I thought then, The hell with it, I am going to let myself be me. I will give them the interview, and I will do it as if it would be their loss not to hire me. I was going to go in there and have fun. If I got the job, good; if not, oh well.

I could no longer let what the interviewers did or did not do determine how I felt about myself. I had convinced myself that I had been as good at what I did as anybody who did it, and if they could not see it, too bad. When the day of the interview came, I, as usual, showed up thirty minutes early. When I arrived, I was greeted by a charming young lady as I introduced myself. She asked me to have a seat, and I did. It was an open room with chairs, and there were two other fellows waiting as well. She called the first fellow up and began the interview with him. This was sort of an open-air-type deal. I and the other fellow had the advantage of hearing the questions that she asked. I suppose she did what she could with the accommodations she had.

The first guy, I thought, was unprepared and did not have ready answers to the questions. He did not even bring a hard copy of his résumé with him, and she had asked us to do so. His interview was short, and I was sure he was eliminated. On to the second guy. He had some of the answers but not all, and he seemed to just slouch in the chair and did not seem too thrilled to be interviewed. I listened carefully and took in all the questions she asked to use to my advantage in my interview. Soon, his interview was over as well. Now it was my turn, and I thought, Show time.

She thanked me for waiting, and she shuffled some things on her desk. I noticed two things: a picture of a young boy, maybe seven, and a certificate for a Six Sigma class with her name on it. Before the interview started, I asked her where she went to get the certificate. She told me, and I then asked her, "Do you have much use for it in your line of work?"

She told me that it was not for that job but where she thought she was heading. I then asked her if she intended to go into a lean manufacturing plant at some point. She said she did not know when but at some point, yes. I then asked her if she had any practice in using the lean techniques. She said no; she had not. I then followed with "It is an effective business tool, but you have to be willing to do some hard things from a management standpoint."

She then asked, "How so?"

I said it was my experience that lean manufacturing meant one thing really, the elimination of wasted time, wasted materials, wasted movement, and wasted labor. This was what it was geared to do: save the company money. It was used to dig out poor practices, organize things, and streamline operations by decreasing the labor force to maximize profit. I said, "If you intend to use it in a management role, then you are going to have to harden your heart. I know you already deal with people and their problems here at the staffing agency, but it is different here. When someone does not show up or the employer is not overly happy with someone, you just pick up the phone and send somebody else. The workers you send out most of the time are not key positions and can be filled by anyone. That means you have a pool to pull from.

I had her attention now. When you begin to learn lean principles, nobody ever tells you about the human aspect of the techniques you are learning. I went on to tell her more. "When you are in a setting where your workers are trained for key positions, they become part of a matrix. The idea is to eliminate the weakest links and to cross-train employees so that no one employee has you over a barrel, because only they know that one special job. That leaves you as an employee with no bargaining chips. So, let's say that you go through the training process, and you see that one of your older employees cannot learn a couple of the jobs that the others can. Now sales are down, and you need to increase profits. You now see that you can eliminate that employee and still get the job done by using cheap labor in that are not key positions and rotating people to cover that position." I asked, "Are you with me so far?"

She said, "Yes," and asked me to continue.

"Okay, here is one problem. Let us say this employee has been with the company a great number of years and has been there almost every day since they were hired and on time as well. Now this employee, although not as skilled as the others, has been very loyal to the company. Now can you, in good conscience, sit in front of this employee and get rid of them? Let us say that you cared for this person and knew they were a good person. When the tears start to flow, can you hold yours back and send that person packing? It is not an easy task but one that comes with the territory when you apply these principles."

She said she saw what I meant. She said, "You sound as if you speak from having to do this."

I answered that I had, and I assured her, it was not easy. I said, "There is another tool that comes with it too. The point system is another tool that goes hand and hand with the lean system. I see you have a picture of a handsome young fellow on your desk."

She said it was her son.

"I, from looking at him, can see he looks to be a healthy young lad."

She said he was.

I told her, "You are blessed. Some people are not so lucky. May I give you an example of the point system where it seems unfair?"

She asked me to please go on.

I preceded to tell her that when using the point system, it was intended to keep your employees at work and on time. This is so there are set parameters to keep no-shows and lateness in check. But now say one of your employees is a single parent and their kid had an illness. And it kept that kid out of school sometimes, not every week but a lot. It is just enough to make them leave early here and there and miss on a regular basis. Now they cannot file FMLA because the illness does not require them to be off for an extended period. They don't have money for a sitter. What's more, they need every dime because they are trying to get by. So that person does not want to be away from work but must be. Now according to the point system, that person has gathered enough points from leaving early and staying home with that child that you must fire that person. What are you going to do? If you don't follow through with the firing, the rest of the employees can use that as an example to get them off the hook. And in many cases, the point system does not apply to management. This furthers the gap between employees and management. It is as if there is one set of rules for management and one for hourly employees. Now what would you do given that problem? Could you fire that employee?"

She looked at me and said she honestly didn't know.

I said, "Then you see now the difference in practices on paper and practices in the real world where human emotions are involved."

She agreed that she now knew something she did not before.

I then said, "I am sorry I took us off our path, and my conversation has drifted from the interview." I continued, "I guess we should begin the interview now."

She said there was no need to be sorry, as she had learned something from what I had said.

I then said, "I am glad to be of service to you."

She said, "Okay, let's get started and get this interview done."

I said, "Fire away!"

She asked me the normal questions, and I gave very definitive answers and expounded on some of them. She liked them all, and she asked one I had not heard. She asked when I thought I was late for work. If I was to be at work at 8:00 a.m., when would I consider myself late?

I asked her what time I showed up today for our appointment. She replied I was thirty minutes early. I said that unless something bad happens, I like being early. I also told her, "When you are a little early, you can kind of see what's going on and what your day might be like."

She asked one last question at the end of the interview. She wanted to know what my weakness was. I said if I had one, it would be I tend to get into my work too much and get to the point of obsessing about it. I go over things in my mind of how I could have done something better or quicker. I have a hard time shutting off my motor. She liked that answer as well.

She then told me, "I will tell you this because I think you are just what they are looking for. The company is a dairy plant, and only ten people will be interviewed. I am going to send you over in the next day or so. I will tell you when. Be ready to go, and dress nice. I think you will take an aptitude test and go from there, but I think they will love you."

I said, "Great!"

She assured me that I would hear from her the next day. I felt good about it and went on home. But remember, I had heard this all before, so I took it with a grain of salt.

Two days went by and no call. I called back and did not reach her. I talked to her counterpart who had no clue who I was and really did not care, other than to tell me she was not in. I told her about what was said and about the test, and she told me the best she could figure there was a holdup on the dairy company's end. I then thought it was another dead end. I had done my best, and I would go on looking. Then that afternoon, she called me. I was to go take the test on a Friday. I thanked her for the opportunity, and she wished me well.

I decided to ride by the address I was given to see if it was the place I thought it was. It was, and you wouldn't believe this, but you cannot make it up. It was the dairy plant that I worked at for about two months almost thirty years ago. It was the same building. The name of the company had changed, but it was the same place. It was less than two miles from where I grew up and less than two miles from where I had spent twenty-five years of my life at the coffee plant. Weird but true.

The day of the test came, and I and nine others assembled at the gate. We appeared to be from a variety of backgrounds. While we waited, I mingled and asked questions of the others. I found that there were four college grads, two who were working on their degrees, a couple of young folks who had worked at some of the local factories, and then one fellow who might have been my age. I don't know where his background was; I did not get that far before we were escorted to where we would take the test.

We were seen into a conference room and asked to present our identification. We were asked to fill out an information form, and then we were given the test. We were told that there was an hour time limit and that when we were through to bring them to the lady up front.

When I opened the test and began to read it, I could not believe it. The first part of the test was on kosher foods. Now the information you needed was in the reading material that was there with the test, and it was multiple choice. I had a leg up here, because when I was at the coffee plant, in my last five years, it was my job to go around with the rabbi to bless the materials and raw goods. He taught me what to look for and what the materials were supposed to have on them as far as symbols go so that people knew they were kosher. We always gave him two cases of coffee, and we were always kosher. I flew through this part of the test.

The next part was one on ethics and what you would do in this situation and then that, such as a dispute between you and a coworker or maybe you have a problem with management. What would you do if you saw a quality problem and knew that by reporting it, you would slow down production? Or you knew by reporting it someone might lose their job? Obvious answers here. This part of the test I called the "you ought to get this right or else" part.

The next part was math put into questions. You were given basic formulas of production and asked to give answers based on your information. One question, however, was sort of a trick question; if you had been in the manufacturing business much, you would know the answer. When given a formula of how many blends you would make to complete a set order, how many would you do? The problem was there was not really a correct answer on the test. The multiple choices gave you one over or one under. Now you would think to answer over. That was the answer they wanted but not always true. I answered the way I knew they wanted. But wrote this on the back of the paper:

When dealing with a perishable item, if you made too much, it would not stay good in inventory, and then it was a wasted product. The correct answer would have been to adjust the blend to match the order by decreasing the formula to fill the order if this could be done; if it could not, then it was management's choice as to lose product or short the customer. That could sometimes be done through negotiations with the customer to give them a deal on the next shipment. Adjusting the formula if the flavor profile could be maintained to complete the order without wasted materials or product was the answer.

I finished first and then took the time to go back over my answers again. I still finished first. I took my test up to the lady and sat back down. The way they had us parked outside, I needed to wait for some of the others to finish so I could leave. When they were done, I went outside and talked to a couple of the guys who had taken the test. We exchanged numbers and did the whole networking thing. I went home.

On the way home, I received a sad call. My wife's brother had passed away, and my niece said that her other brother had tried to call her but could not reach her. They didn't know the details pertaining to his death, but the family needed to do something, as he had no wife or family in South Carolina where he had lived. I was asked to call my wife and break the news to her. I did and wished that I would not have had to. I wish I could have told her in person, but she was at work at the time. When she arrived home, I consoled her as best I could. Her brother from Louisiana began the drive over the next morning, and we were to ride to South Carolina to make the arrangements.

Just about the time he arrived, and we were on our way out the door to go, the phone rang. It was the dairy company. They said that based on my score from the test and my résumé, they wanted an interview with me and HR. I asked when, and they said tomorrow. It was Thursday. I quickly told them of what was going on and begged for Monday for the interview. The lady on the other end said, "I don't know. Hold on."

She left the phone and came back. She said they would interview at 9:00 a.m., Monday morning. I told her thank you and said I was sorry about my situation. She said it was ok and that I had scored perfect on the test and was the only one. She followed by saying they were really interested in me. I thanked her again, and we went to South Carolina to take care of the arrangements.

Monday found me at their gate again dressed and ready. I was prepared and still thought it was so weird to be back someplace I had worked at thirty years before. I was met by the guard, and he told me where to go. I did notice one thing: it was now so much nicer a place. Everything was new and clean. The old building had been renovated and had a great new look. I went to the office desk and introduced myself. The lady behind the desk said for me to have a seat, that they would be with me in a minute. I looked around and saw they had a showcase that had all their products in it. I had studied up on them. The majority of what they produced was soy milk. It was a very nice office and even had samples of their product for you to drink while you waited.

Soon I heard high heels coming down the stairs. I was greeted by a very tall, beautiful woman wearing very high heels. She was nice and friendly. She was the HR person there. She had to be over six feet tall already without the heels. I am a short guy, so she towered over me. I was shown to her office and asked to have a seat. In just a minute or two, we were joined by the production manager. She was a young lady, maybe between twenty-seven and thirty. She, I could tell, was very intelligent and bright. I could tell this by the way she talked. One other thing I could tell was she had a sense of humor.

Once we were all seated, I presented each one of them with a hard copy of my résumé. Then the interview began. I was first asked to tell them about myself. Now these ladies knew their stuff, so I poured it on thicker and thicker. I could see by the look on the production manager's face that the more I knew about food and beverage manufacturing the better she liked it. So, I let it all hang out.

I then began to answer their questions one by one. One would ask a question and then the other. One question was since I had been a supervisor, would I be okay with not being the man? I answered that I had not been the man in the last three years, and I had twenty years of not being the man. I said that I found that once I took the other job with my buddy, it was a humbling experience. It was hard to go from running the show to just making it go. But I would be fine letting someone else take the reins.

The next questions were pretty much the standard ones I had heard in all my other interviews. Then they got to the one about what I had been doing with myself these eighteen months I had been off. I told them the standard things, such as looking for work and taking care of my mother's affairs, and then, out of the clear blue sky, I said, "I have also written a book."

That surprised them. It was for sure something that they had never heard at an interview before. They asked what it was about. Now this is the book you are reading currently. I had written two, but this is the one I talked about. I told them it was sort of a book based on my life in manufacturing. It was what had led me to the point that I was at and what I had been through along the way. It was about what it was like to be fifty years old, looking for a job, and starting over.

They then asked when it would be out. I said, "It is not finished yet. I have one more chapter to write. The last chapter is where you hire me, and I live happily ever after."

They almost fell out of their seats.

I then said, "I hope it is out in the spring."

I had not just hit a home run—this was a grand slam. The statement was direct, and it was "If you don't hire me, you are missing out." It amused them as well as showed confidence.

The last question was the tall HR lady's. She asked me this: "Now that we have heard everything about you. Tell me why we should hire Rick Johnson?"

I looked at her squarely and said, "You don't know by now?"

The production manager laughed out loud despite herself, and so did the HR lady. The production manager said she had sat through hundreds of interviews and that was the best answer to that question she had ever heard. I followed quickly with "The real reason you should hire me is I am bringing twenty-five years of food and beverage manufacturing to the table and a whole truckload of work ethic that you may not find in a younger employee."

They were very impressed. They said that concluded the interview and if they went forward, I would receive a call from the staffing agency.

I thanked them for their time and for rescheduling the interview because of my circumstances. They said it was okay; they understood. I then told them I hoped to hear from them soon. I left.

I thought I had done something different this time, and it had worked. I had become at once confident and a little arrogant as to feel like it was their loss not to hire me.

As I drove home, I rode by my old neighborhood. It had changed. It seemed so small now. The yards looked cramped and tight. When I was a kid, it seemed as big as the world, just in my own backyard. It had run down so much. The once-manicured yards and freshly painted homes were now boarded up and had graffiti on them. There were folks on street corners trying to wave me down. I did not stop and wheeled on through. My mom had moved out of there ten years before, and I could not believe the transformation. Then I drove back out and went on my way home.

As I drove, my trip took me right past my old place of work. I took the turn and drove to the end of the road where our once-thriving plant was at. There were a few cars in the lot. After shutting us down, the company found out they indeed would have to keep the building because it sat on their lease. So, they kept it, and now it was just an old warehouse. I looked at it and thought it was so sad. People had raised their families and paid for their homes with money that came from that plant. They had fed and clothed them, and it gave the community livelihood. Now it was a warehouse with a couple of people manning it. I guess things just never stay the same. I still cannot let go of it though.

Had the company listened to the employees who could see all this coming, we would have still been there. We would still be thriving and contributing to the neighborhood. It was all for naught though, and I guess I will never let it go. It is a wound that just won't heal. After sitting and looking at it for a little while, I remembered my first day there and my last. I thought of the people I had met and of whose lives I had been a part for twenty-five years. I thought of all the ones who had passed on and gone. I thought how it was that even though we were so much like a family, we were all doing our own things now. As I had known we would, we all drifted apart. People who work together, though they might be mad at each other at times, have a connection. They are still on the same team and must work together to get things done. It is a bond that is quickly broken, in most cases, when the team is dismantled.

I had always hoped it would be like my mom's work. For many years, they had a reunion of the old workers at her department store. That went on until many of them passed away. Our plant, however, had been pushed apart by the system, and we were made to turn on each other. We were put in survival mode, one against the other. It had driven a stake between us all, and I was a part of it. This saddened me deeply because beyond it all, I really cared for all the people there.

Only the system pushed me to feel the way I did then. I had no recourse, no way to stop it other than leave what I had fought for all those years. I felt deep sorrow at how it all played out. After taking one last look, I told myself I would never pull down that road again and I would leave it behind.

CHAPTER 28

THE LOTTERY

The next day came, and about 10:00 a.m., I received a call. It was the lady at the staffing agency. I could hardly believe what I was hearing. I was told I was hired! I was also told that I was being hired outright and not going through the staffing agency. I had done well through the whole process, and now I would be employed. The way this went down was amazing. They had started by running the ad online and in the paper. They had accepted over a thousand applications and résumés. There were over five hundred people who showed up at their gate the day of open applications.

Out of the thousand, they sorted through and picked five hundred. Then their HR department picked one hundred from the five hundred. They then sent the hundred to be interviewed by the staffing agency. Ten were picked from the hundred to go and take the aptitude test. Out of those ten, the top five scores were hired to go to work. I considered myself lucky and blessed.

I was told of the next step, which would be background screening and the standard drug test. They told me when and where, wished me luck, and congratulated me. I thanked her so much for picking me and told her what it meant to me and the wife. I hung up the phone and sat there, just looking into space. Had I really been hired? Was this true? Did somebody see something in me finally? I was overjoyed. I called the wife and told her, and we planned a night out. I informed my family and friends I was going back to work. Everyone was happy.

Now I am back at work in the same building I was in over thirty years ago. I hope to have better results. I have given up for the time being on going back to management. I will try to settle in and be an operator. I have taken this road, and it was not as if I had a choice. This was the only road that was offered. I will make the best of it and hope that the machine's pace does not kill me. It has been a long journey to this point, and it has been a roller-coaster ride of emotions. I find myself once again in hours I did not want and on a schedule that conflicts with my home life. It, however, is a job and, believe you me, one I needed at this time in my life.

My advice to you is this, my dear readers. Learn a trade. Those jobs are the last to go. To start with, make yourself invaluable to your place of work. Make it to where you will only have to leave if the place shuts down. Try to be there as much as possible and contribute as much as you can. Be prepared to lose your job. Have an emergency fund. Save that income tax check; don't spend it until you see your place of business is secure. If you find yourself without a job now in this economy, you will have needed to stash as much money as you can. The job search can take a long time. You are now competing against thousands, and they have the same skills as you. Some even better.

Keep positive, and never let your interviewer make you change how you feel about yourself. Be confident; don't go to interviews acting beaten up. Be prepared; know as much as possible about the job you are going for before showing up for the interview. Ask about the attire for the interview. Walk in like you own the place, and never let them see you don't. Be yourself; that is who they are hiring. Keep in the back of your mind that if they don't hire you, the next one will. You are there to do your best and be secure that you did even if you're not hired.

Your dream job may be out there or not right now. Be open to what is for right now. Take what you can get when you can get it. There is nothing in life that says later when things get better and the job market changes, you cannot make a change. Gone are the days when employees are hired for life, and so are the days when you must stay in one place for life. It comes down to a swap: you give them a hard day's work, and they give you a paycheck. Beyond that, it is all fair in today's working world.

If you find yourself without a job, try to stay active. Those extra pounds come quickly when your off work. Walk, or do something to keep moving, anything—just don't vegetate. Take time to do projects and stuff you would not have otherwise had time to do. Keep your job search going but stop and smell the roses a little bit. More than likely, you will work most of your life.

Why not try to enjoy a little time off, if you're in good health and have funds to live? Most people say that when you retire, there is only one big event left. All too often, I have seen people retire, and then they are gone. Their whole life is spent in pursuit of a paycheck. Remember what my dad said in chapter 1. Dad always said, "Once you get the first one, you will always want one." It may be a good time to reflect on what you have and haven't done. If you want that degree, go get it. I wish now I would have. It could not hurt you and might get you a little further down the line. Try something you always wanted to do like paint or write a book, something you would have done long ago, if given the time. Make use of the time; don't let it slip by. When you go back to work, there may be little extra time for you to pursue something out of the norm. Travel a little if you can. Spend time with loved ones and strengthen those bonds now that you have time.

Make sure if you are older that you have secured yourself some type of insurance. If you are a younger person reading this, then maybe you can wing it until something comes along. If you are older and maybe you are not as healthy as all that, then you better find something somewhere. One three-day stay in the hospital without insurance could ruin you or at the very least deplete your nest egg. Even if it is something cheap, if it is all you can afford, at least it is better than nothing. If it pays a little, a drop in the bucket is better than a dry one. If you are a young person, you may be at the age when you can roll the dice and make it until you have insurance through a company. Even still the statement applies to you as well.

Try your best to stay away from the credit cards. It is all too tempting to reach for the plastic when you are in a tight spot. Roll those pennies and sell anything that you don't need. Yard sale it, garage sale it, or see if a friend who is in a better situation may want to buy it. If you have old gold or silver that just sits in the drawer of the jewelry box and has for ages, sell it. It is better to make use of it in that way than just let it sit there. Why add to your credit card bill? There may be emergencies that call for you to use the card but save it for a last resort. When you get back to work, you want your credit rating intact. Any bills that you make while unemployed will be there with interest when you go back to work.

There is one other thing: if you get laid off and your spouse, life partner, or live-in or whatever is still working, think how they feel now. They are now carrying the load. The pressure just got turned up on them. Now they must bring home the bacon. The pressure is on for them to keep their jobs. They feel even more obligated to do what they can to see to it that the household keeps going.

And in some cases, even their bosses knowing you were laid off will turn up the heat. They now know that they need their jobs even more, and all their bargaining chips are gone. Before, they may have thought if I push this person too hard, their significant other makes pretty good money, and they may walk out. That option is now gone. I am not saying that is every boss situation, but you can see how it could happen. Some will be sympathetic to their situation and try to help out by giving them extra overtime or surprise bonuses.

So do for that person if you are home. Take the house and yard chores on for yourself and let them just work. Take as much off them as possible, and know they appreciate it, even if it is something you are not used to doing. Just think, years ago, only one person worked to support a household. It is your turn now to shoulder more responsibility for the house and all the things that go with it. You may even find yourself liking it. Believe me, when your high-pressure point of the day is dealing with the little old ladies at the grocery store hitting you in the heels with a grocery cart, life isn't that bad. Think about the person still working and what their day is like.

If the shoe is on the other foot and you find yourself married or living with a person who is laid off, be supportive. In some cases, maybe that person has dealt with unemployment before. Maybe it is not new to them; maybe they have dealt with it lots of times or maybe a few. They might have a different outlook on the situation. It is always easier sailing charted waters. But let us say it is someone like me who has only had two jobs in almost thirty years. It is a scary world out there to people who fit these criteria.

You find yourself almost fifty or fifty and now what? It is a situation that you may not be familiar with. Now more than ever, you need someone to tell you it will be all right no matter what. I have been so lucky to be married to a person who has stood behind me and has helped pick me up every single time. I know it is not easy for them to do it in some cases. They are stressed too. But if the person you are with is indeed doing all they can to go back to work, then support them. When they hit that brick wall out there, somebody needs to be around to put ice on that bump. There were many times when I felt angry and mad at myself, and I thought the whole world had turned on me. I always knew, though, that no matter what, my wife would never turn her back on me. In that fact, I did take great comfort.

If you are unfortunate in the fact that your partner used this time to make a change in their life, then good riddance. If they decided this was too much for them to handle and bailed out, it is better you found out now. Use them for inspiration. Get downright mad-dog mean with determination. Make up your mind you will come through it, and when you do, you will be smiling more than they ever saw you smile and be happier than they could ever have made you. Find a person who will stick with you to the bitter end. If they want back in after the job situation improves, don't just say no but hell no! I have seen this happen to friends of mine. I have also heard of this happening to people, and I feel for them. It is bad enough to be out of work but out of love also? That's rough territory for the soundest of souls.

If there is not a husband or wife or love of your life to stand behind you, then rely on your friends and family. Always remember, if they are still around, Mom and Pop are your best friends and then brothers and sisters and then friends. My mom encouraged me every day with things she would say to make me feel better about myself and my situation. She told me never to doubt who I was or what I could do, just because somebody's company did not have the business to keep me on. It was the economy to blame and not my worth as an employee. She kept telling me after every disappointment that it was okay. Sometimes she would turn on the sour grapes routine and say, "Son, you really deserve to work someplace better anyway. Those folks are just missing out." I know she would just say things to make me feel better, but it always felt good hearing it. Confide in your family and friends and reassure them that you will be there when they need someone as well.

Well, as I close this long story, I hope that anyone who reads this can gather something good out of it. I have told you my story thus far, and I hope you have been entertained. I have gone through every emotion in this book. I have shared my victories and my defeats, my ups and downs. I really don't think you have to have been in manufacturing to understand this; it is everybody's story. We all have had challenges and hard times to deal with. I have learned many things over the course of this book and many things about myself while writing it. You see, as I wrote this, I was living it or had lived it. It has been my escape, even though the world that it is in is based in is reality. Get it?

To clarify this book, I write it as it was. Was I the hero of my story? Yes. Are we not all the heroes of our own stories? Was I the villain? I would like to think not. But that is up to the reader's interpretation. There may have been those under my supervision who thought so. Was I a victim? Of circumstance? Yes, at times I was. But in general, at any time in my twenty-five years at the plant, I could have made the choice to leave and did not. In that, I was not a victim but by my own design. Loyalty is a double-edged sword. It may save you when you are under attack, and your loyalty is all that is keeping you from losing your job. Then you can be so loyal you will take being passed over for promotions and take demotions and beatings in the workplace, harming yourself. You then can find yourself falling on that same sword. It is a tricky thing. Or at least then it was. You can care so much for a coworker you put yourself in a bad situation for loyalty.

And also, these folks back at the plant, many have passed on, and in 2025, the place will have been shut down for twenty years. But no matter what I have written, I loved most of these people. We were family, and that is something I don't see anymore. I don't want anyone to be disparaged in the writing of this book or their respective roles in it. I wrote it how I saw it and lived it. And if the shoe does fit, you must wear it. But know this, too: I didn't need a shoehorn to make it fit you. This shall be a question that you must ask yourself.

So now I have made my ninety days as I close this book, and I am proud to say I am still employed. I have worked seven days a week for over fifty days now. Talk about making up lost ground. I work with a diverse group of folks again, and I see things there that I saw when I worked at the coffee plant. I see the system creeping in, and an atmosphere being created, one I hoped I would not see. It is one where it is us against them, as far as one shift against the other and one employee against another. I know I should not say so, but I am warning my co-workers. This is not good for anybody. Do not let yourself be pushed into a situation where people you cared about are now your rivals. It might be or might not be, but I know one thing for sure: I will never let a system divide or change who or what I am or harden me again.

Oh yeah, before I go, there is one other thing about this place that I never had before. This is a new one for me.

Can you say union?

ACKNOWLEDGMENTS

I want to thank my wife, Debbie, for standing behind me and my family as well. I want to thank Bluto, my Great Dane, who has lain at my feet and kept me company through the entire writing of this book and the whole time I was unemployed. I want to dedicate this book to my father, Doyle A. Johnson, and my mother, Betty L. Johnson, who instilled in me my work ethic, my determination when put to task, my will to keep going when the landscape looks bleak, and my courage to try to do what's right and protect my own heart, which is at times difficult.

I also am grateful to C.J. Powell Jr, "Pop," who has also passed on and was always a mentor to me. He embodied the resilience of what it is to be a working man. He mastered iron and steel and molded it to his will, which was as strong as the iron and steel he worked with.

And thank you to God Almighty, who has seen fit to pull me out of one hole then the next. In every aspect of my life, he has been there, through everything—mentally, physically, emotionally, and spirituality. No matter what, he has pulled me through. For some odd reason, I am still here against all odds. I think he just wants to see what I will do next. And one of those things is to honor him. Thank God.

ABOUT THE AUTHOR

I was born on the Westside of Jacksonville Florida. Where my wife and myself still reside. I am a late generation Baby Boomer. Born a very small child with an underdog mentality. I had an older and younger brother. We were raised by two loving hard working parents. Who excelled at their perspective trades. They majored in sweat and grit. And a commitment to no matter the job be the very best one doing it.

I graduated from Paxon Sr. High A Golden Eagle. I have been working since I was 12. This was my way to earn money if I wanted any. Cutting yards,washing cars,raking yards. Any job that grown folks would trust me to do. It was a bad time for our family. As in 1972 my father suffered a heart attack. At that time the knowledge of treating the heart was limited. This put our family on one income with bills based on two. It was 6 months before my father could return to full time work. It was a struggle that took years to recover from. This was motivation early on to find ways to earn money. And as soon as a work permit was attainable I was working legally at age 14.

I tried a variety of blue collar jobs. I settled on manufacturing. Food and Beverage in particular. I excelled at it. The more physical the job the better for me. I had from age 13 I began to lift weights to offset my small size. So I was ready for hard work. I also did spend 5 years in management. By the way with nothing in my arsonal but blood and guts and a mind that allowed me to think days in advance to the minute.

I have learned most concepts of Lean Manufacturing. And have been in on the implementation of these concepts. And in working within the parameters set forth as a blue collar worker.

I am now retired. Having lived through so many things. Adversity and myself are not strangers. I managed to at 50 to navigate a massive recession at an undesirable age for blue collar workers.

I live to the best of my abilty with limited means. And my story is not rare. I would say at my age now it is the norm. But I was fortunate to have married someone who shared my work ethic and desire for a peaceful life. And together never wavered.

But who am I? Who is this author? I am a man wanting to tell you a story. I am a man who has survived and thrived through every one of lifes challenges. Mentally, physiaclly and emotinally.

I am a reflection of Late Generation Baby Boomers. A champion for Generation X. I am a path finder for Millinueals. I am Blue Collar. I am Richard A. Johnson.

Milton Keynes UK
Ingram Content Group UK Ltd.
UKHW021425111224
452348UK00007B/446